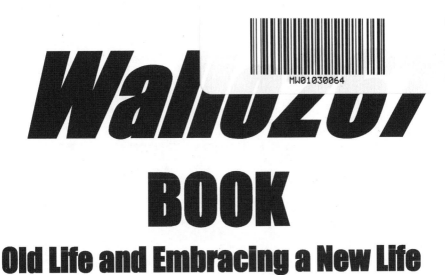

BOOK

Old Life and Embracing a New Life

TABLE OF CONTENTS

CHAPTER 22   REFORMED

CHAPTER 1
FIRST DAY OUT

I was released from a state jail in Northumberland County, Pennsylvania, on the morning of Saturday, February 18, 2017.
Not quite, though.
I am on parole until 2048 even though I physically stood on the other side of the prison's gates. Allow me to explain what this implies to all of you.
A judge will impose a minimum and maximum punishment on an individual found guilty of a crime. The minimum sentence is the amount of time you must serve before the parole board will even consider granting you an early release. The longest term you can serve before fulfilling your obligation to society is known as your maximum sentence. I was sentenced to thirteen and a half to twenty-seven years in prison for armed robbery in 2002, when I was twenty-three years old. I served fifteen of those years since my sentence had a set minimum of thirteen and a half years, unlike a determinate, where the sentence imposed by a judge cannot be reviewed or amended by a parole board or any other agency. However, I consented to serve a 2048 parole term when I was given an early release. In Pennsylvania, the parole period is double the number of years that the offender was actually serving their sentence. I am thus not precisely a "free man."
That's why, in my all-black Nike sweatsuit and matching black huaraches that my younger brother Troy sent me before I left, I could hardly feel the brisk air. That was the scariest day of my life, even though I was glad to be wearing clothes I wasn't given by the state. Because I was on parole, even a minor infraction may cost me my brittle freedom. In addition, I felt I had to live up to the fifteen years of letters and phone conversations I had sent and received from my mother, my grandmother Nanny, and other family members pledging that this time would be different.
"How are you feeling?" Latifah, my sister from a previous mother, inquired multiple times while driving to fetch me.
"Excellent as hell!" I answered.
We stopped at a McDonald's on the two and a half hour journey back to North Philadelphia from the prison. I devoured an Egg McMuffin,

hash browns, and a medium orange juice, relishing every bite. At Walmart, our next destination, I was able to get genuine razors for shaving my face. We arrived at Nanny's house while it was still light outside. She was in the living room, hugging me as soon as I went in. It made me think of that small guy who used to eat grits and scrapple and fiddle with the television's antennae so he could watch Saturday morning cartoons with my elder brother, Stevie.

"I'm very glad you're back home," Nanny remarked. Nanny pulled me from her hug and looked directly into my eyes. There was a tangible grief beneath her mask of happiness. Her expression of dread was telling: "I hope you get this right."

Nanny was perfectly entitled to feel this way about me. I had been in and out of jails, police precincts, juvenile detention centres, and prisons for the previous twenty-seven years. I had committed drug sales, people-stealing, and dropping out of school. It turned out to be more of the same, even though I had promised her that this would be the last time. My powerlessness met Nanny's scepticism since I knew there was nothing I could do at that particular moment to make her feel differently about the way I had behaved in the past. My deeds would now have to speak for themselves, louder than words.

Throughout that homecoming week, I was favoured with a few bucks here and some garments there by neighbours. I had roughly $1,000 between the money I had saved up from working different jobs while incarcerated and the money I received from friends and family. As I sat there staring at the money, it occurred to me that I had spent the most of my life behind bars not just because I took risks but also because I frequently bet against myself.

I gambled with two valuable assets—your time and your life—devoting a significant portion of my life to discovering the quickest path to financial gain. When you lose that gamble, you cannot get your money back. I would be lying if I claimed that I had never won any hands, but I would also be lying if I denied that the losses I suffered after being apprehended far outweighed any wins I had while living a life of crime. Within the first three years following their release, 64.7% of formerly imprisoned individuals in Pennsylvania commit new crimes. Approximately 50% of the recidivism occurs within a mere 18 months of discharge. There are two ways to look at this: either playing the numbers or realising that the odds are stacked against me. The goal at this stage is to never return if my chances of reoffending decrease with each year I serve my sentence.

Blessed to be alive, I sat on my bed and felt very embarrassed of the time that was lost forever. However, for the first time in my life, I was also filled with hope because I had a chance to do something I had never done before: place a bet on myself.

Can't nobody fuck with me, I thought to myself, if I could channel the hustler's enthusiasm I brought to stealing, dealing, and robbing into inspiring others to give it their all in order to realize their full potential while remaining out of trouble.

CHAPTER 2
NANNY

My nanny is LOIS PEEPLES, MY MOTHER'S MOTHER. Nanny was the head of bottling inventory at ERNO Products Company for thirty-one years. Nanny was the definition of a diligent worker—during those thirty-one years, she missed just forty-one days.

I have never had a stronger attachment than I have with Nanny. She is thurl, which is Philly slang for "thorough"; she is both tough and soft like a cloud. Even though she is smart and well-versed in the game, even after we spend hours talking, she still seems genuinely interested in anything I have to say, almost as if she is hearing it all for the first time. Standing at roughly five three, she has always been stunning, with skin as smooth as mahogany and butter. She would identify the model, shape, and size of any bottle style that was placed within a mile of her gaze. She would snap, "That's a Cylinder, shorty neck, thirty-millimetre cap." The foundation of the family is Nanny. When none else did, she still had faith in me.

She was raised in an era where girls who played athletics were labelled as "tomboys," and her first career goals were to coach women's basketball teams or teach physical education. I include these things to help you understand that Nanny wasn't your typical grandmother—she didn't wear slippers and a muumuu. She wore sneakers and jeans every day.

Nanny is a kind individual. Nanny is compassionate. Nanny is kind. Nanny takes initiative. However, my mother used to make me grits with either bacon or scrapple on the side when I was around five or six, and that was one of my favourite things ever. That was the ultimate poo of all time. Sitting at the table used to make me happy. She cooked the dishes in these tough, black skillets that she had.

Summertime days spent with my grandma include some of my most treasured and early memories, prior to feelings of shame and rage. To me, Nanny's house felt like a playground. When I was there, there was nothing I couldn't imagine and make happen. It was a row house off Thirteenth Street, of a respectable size. Nanny's La-Z-Boy was on the first floor, where she watched her game shows.

When I was younger, I remember being upstairs and acting like a ghetto superhero. I was only wearing my tighty-whities and a towel around my neck like a cape as I jumped from bed to bed and crashed into the walls and furniture. I could hear Nanny preparing dinner for us in the kitchen downstairs. She could have something for me to do, so I was hesitant to go down and ask what she was preparing. When it came to completing the tasks she assigned you, Nanny didn't mess around. She would not think twice to take out her three-inch-thick cowboy belt and give us sibling whoops like we were Indiana Jones if my siblings and I misbehaved. Oh no, the welts seem like they were from yesterday. One licking round and you'd swear you were pistol-whipped.

Wallace, why is there so much noise up there? Now please get your butt down here! Nanny yelled. I was moving so quickly down the stairs that I didn't even consider the possibility that I wouldn't have a piece of clothing to protect me if I got light up. I was really startled when I noticed the metal buckle.

Indeed, Nanny. I was just having fun," I stumbled, panting from upstaging the idiot. Nanny burst out laughing after glancing at me.

"Boy, you better hurry up and take a shower, put on some damn clothes, and get ready to eat. She was only able to get a few words out before she burst out laughing. She added, laughing, "I'm making your favourite, apple pound cake." I knew then and there that I wanted to offer her everything if I could.

Nanny always had the ideal response ready. Nanny could answer any question I had about life, ladies, or anything else. She would respond to almost anything, no questions asked, exactly the way she enjoyed her whisky. She had lovely brown skin, and there was always something about the fragrance of warm scotch that made me feel fuzzy.

When Nanny was three or ten years old, we used to take her tan Monte Carlo station wagon down to her hometown of Seaford, Virginia, for summer visits with Great-Grandma Lee, also known as Liola. I used to think of a million questions just to hear the tone of her voice on those long journeys down to the countryside.

"Do you think I'm smart, Nanny?" Once, out of genuine interest, I inquired.

"I do, of course, sweetie. Like your grandmother, you possess intelligence and sharpness. But you just don't like to act appropriately," she shot back, shaking her head softly. "Wally-Oh, you're going to have to start behaving appropriately and conducting yourself in public and at school, or it will eventually catch up with you. Her voice would trail off with a little crackle, as if she could see the road I was on better than the twisting I-95 in front of her.

Growing up, my mother was more like my sister because she was young, just twenty-two, when she gave birth to me. I therefore thought of Nanny as my mother at the time. I was ignorant for a long time about the importance of age in parenting and how, even after having us, our parents are constantly attempting to define who they are. Despite her best efforts, my mother's love for me was not as deep or affectionate as that of my grandmother and great-grandmother. Perhaps it had to do with my mother growing up beneath the dismal, Gotham City-like Philadelphia clouds and away from the warm peach-country skies; perhaps it was just because she was still a young woman herself.

I was able to see how different life may be from those travels to Virginia. Those drives down would never cease to astonish me with how different the trees were in all their hues, sizes, and shapes. During the long stretch of southern miles, the light would reflect off bright yellow, orange, and green leaves, making them dance and wave at us as we passed. It would then bounce off the car's hood and land in my lap. I would observe every little thing. The clouds in Philadelphia appeared to linger well behind us, and the air was as crisp and pure as the apples in Nanny's pound cake. Even for a short weekend, getting away from the city brought me clarity and tranquillity. I was able to appreciate the beauty of the surrounding environment and the blank canvas that allowed me to visualise anything I wanted under the clear blue sky of the ocean. And most of all, Nanny's chocolate-brown eyes would give me tender glances as I saw them in the rearview mirror.

"Yes, Wally-O." When we got there, those were the first words I would hear, like a melody being sung by an angel. Every time I arrived, Great-Grandma Lee would welcome me with wide arms with the sweetest, brightest smile that could light up the entire town.

You wouldn't believe how quickly I would get used to living in the country.

Great-Grandma Lee would tell me to slow down, boy, as I hurried her back inside the house to gather the ingredients for our well-known sun tea.

I would enthusiastically blurt out, "Granny, we have to hurry before the sun goes down, and we won't be able to make our tea."

"Don't worry, child; you know I always have a pitcher ready for you when you get here," Granny added, her gorgeous smile highlighting her high cheekbones. But after a long commute from the city, it had little to do with the tea or even with being thirsty. It was the collaborative process of creating something, and witnessing my creation come to life to share with all of you.

"Check for mason jars. Check for tea bags. Water, see. And last but not least, sugar, check," I would recite the list of ingredients that needed to be carried outside to the kitchen shed behind the home, making sure to remember everything as I hurried back and forth. A white family whose children Great-Grandma Lee reared constructed her home. To keep a roof over all of our heads, my great-grandmother had to work as someone else's nanny, tending to kids who didn't look like us while her kids waited for her past nightfall.

The long, silver hair of Great-Grandma Lee would sparkle in the sunlight like ornaments on a Christmas tree. When we sat drinking a cool glass of sun tea on the porch at night, Nanny used to comb Granny Lee's hair and oil her scalp. Nanny would divide her hair in half and create two lengthy braids after giving her lustrous locks a massage and some moisture. Her braids hung almost to the floor.

"Granny, how'd you get your hair so long like that?" I enquired.

"Well, it demonstrates my level of wisdom. Furthermore, unlike what they say, we are Geechee people with some Indian ancestry.

When the sun dropped, cats and kittens flocked to the patio. When the sun went down, you could only see two feet away here at Granny Lee's, unlike in the city where streetlamps would light up and offer you some vision in the shadows. If I claimed that I wasn't terrified to death when curled up in the dark with my tiny group of purring cats, I would be lying. It seemed strange, the silence and the stillness. My mind would be racing, with millions of ideas swirling about and nowhere to go. Eventually in life, I learned that the whirling tempests of ideas I was attempting to quiet were actually attention deficit disorder, which was misdiagnosed and left untreated.

Always, the trip back to Philadelphia was bittersweet. We seemed to have spent just enough time together for me to miss jogging on the streets, but never enough time for the associated issues to fade from my memory. I remember being so young and bewildered by the ups and downs in my own mental condition. Since I can remember, I have always known that I want to be the man and that I will do great things to make my family proud. Being Robin Hood from the Hood was my dream. I wanted to be the one with enough money in my pockets to get whatever someone needed. However, I failed to see that I was only a child. That stuff would therefore rip a hole in my chest whenever things became tight at home or pals ran out of money to eat.

My Nanny would frequently tell me, "Baby, when you stop moving, you stop moving." Nanny tried her best to raise me in a way that would benefit me in the long run, even though she knew I was a knucklehead at that point in my life.

However, June 30, 1990 was a unique day. Nanny was the first person they phoned when we got to the precinct. "Oh my God, what in the world have you done?"

My uncle Tommy was sent by her to come get me. I can now appreciate the consequences of a young person being detained. I would be saddened to learn that my eleven-year-old nephew was arrested today, but at the time I had no context for this.

My uncle Tommy isn't homeless now. I used to spend my time in his room at Nanny's house, guy, just kicking back with eight tracks and comedic records featuring everyone from Richard Pryor to Redd Foxx. He would be rolling what he called "reefer," his marijuana, on the tapes. Despite his constant fixing of various things around the area, he remained out of the way. He was the local handyman.

Naturally, Nanny was furious when we returned to her house, but even then, her expression was still showing more fear, despair, and even helplessness. She was still working and trying to hang on to her life at that point; she had not yet retired. My grandfather Charles Vincent Peeples, her husband and a veteran of the military, got his ass up and threw him out of the house when he caught himself lifting his hand to Nanny.

Even though my gorgeous Nanny was strong and punished me severely for stealing the girl's necklace, I already had a strong sense of morality, even if at that moment my head was more powerful than my ass. In less than a month, I would be detained twice more for the identical offences. Nanny would give a headshake.

"I hope you learn before it's too late, but I'm not sure when or what will teach you before then."

11

I was in and out of juvenile jail for a large portion of my youth. I felt nearly like a boxer getting ready for his big bid. But I was unable to defend myself! I attended St. Michael's School for Boys in Tunkhannock, Pennsylvania, for two years, from 1990 to 1992. It was a program designed to give wayward adolescents direction and discipline in the hopes of a successful reintroduction into society, but it was all rubbish. For youngsters like me, the most they ever did was thrust board games in our faces and walk away long enough for us to plan our next criminal adventure. No adult, therapist, or counsellor showed any interest in asking me why I was acting in the way that I was, or what it was about my surroundings that kept pushing me to make the poor choices that would ultimately bring me to ruin. For many of them, this was only a paycheck, and in the not too distant future, they would have a sizable pension.

I didn't even know what anxiety was back then, but I knew I was pissed the fuck off. My anger was always simmering beneath the surface, and I longed to let out all of my fury and yell at them. Simply speak from the heart! Tell it straight to my face! How come? Oh, you believe I'm stupid? You don't bclievc that my fucking independence is worth it! As counsellors jotted down their brief notes and assessments of me, all these clashing sound bits bounced off the walls of my consciousness. Luckily for them, I was unable to express myself fully without worrying about receiving further punishment. As a result, I would uncomfortably stare into space for the duration of our meetings, subconsciously drifting off to sleep.

Quarterly Review of Service Plan
PERIOD COVERED:
June 1991 to August 1991
NAME:
Wallace Peeples
AGE:
12
PRESENTING PROBLEMS/REASON FOR REFERRAL:
Wallace Peeples was referred to St. Michael's Residential Program by Philadelphia County Juvenile Probation. Wallace was adjudicated delinquent on charges of robbery, simple assault, reckless endangerment, and receiving stolen property. It is noted that Wallace Peeples is being handled by the Habitual Offenders Unit of the Philadelphia County Juvenile Probation Department. Wallace was admitted to St. Michael's on 9-19-1990.

Wallace has shown some difficulty in accepting responsibility for his actions. At times, he relies on denial or projection to minimise accountability.

Wallace has demonstrated impulsive behaviours with little thought to the consequences of those behaviours for himself and others.

Wallace seems to be experiencing low self-esteem as manifested in the impaired ability to form appropriate relationships with others, a tendency to be a follower, a lack of goals, and inconsistent motivation for self-improvement.

Wallace appears to resist having limits or structure imposed upon him. He has little insight into the need for order, structure, and accountability.

Wallace is in need of a trusting relationship with adult role models to provide him with emotional support on a consistent basis that will allow him the opportunity to verbalise his feelings.

Quarterly Review of Service Plan
PERIOD COVERED:
7-29-92 to 10-29-92
AREAS OF INTERVENTION:
Wallace has demonstrated impulsive behaviours with little thought to the consequences of these behaviours for himself or others.
METHODOLOGY:
A combination of counselling and behavioural management approaches will be utilised to improve self-control and to provide positive reinforcement for thoughtful, planned behaviours.
GOAL AND TARGET DATE:
Wallace will develop a better ability to consider alternatives and to recognize and consider the consequences of his behaviour.
TARGET DATE:
Ongoing
PERSON(S) RESPONSIBLE:
Wallace
Social Worker
Treatment Team
CURRENT STATUS:
Impulse control on Wallace's part continues to be a major concern. This is no more evident than by Wallace's actions previously noted on the weekend of 8/7 thru 8/9. Wallace's rearrest and reinvolvement in delinquent activity goes to the point that he clearly remains at risk for poorly planned and poorly thought-out kinds of activities.

CHAPTER 3
IMAGINARY PLAYER

VERONICA SMITH was her name. Each of us was fourteen years old. Uptown Philadelphia was her home. She was a stunning girl with fair skin. I had my first taste of love from that girl—she was the first to make me cry. I'm out here boosting and taking clothes right now. Between one of my tenures at Vision Quest, this occurred in 1993. I was back in juvenile detention when I wasn't on probation.

She was with her girls, and I was with one of the homies. I then approached her. Being one of those guys who could never stop laughing, I said something like, "Damn Slimmy, what's up?"

She chuckled and gave me a perfunctory glance.

I don't even know you, boy!

I was around older guys like Stevie, who had a mouthpiece, knew how to dress well, understood how to get with ladies, and all of that. They were fully aware of when, how, and what to say.

However, I wasn't really a player. I was a figment of my imagination. a participant by default. My stepfather Hip laid me down with all the classics, so I was listening to Ice-T, Special Ed, and 2 Live Crew. I was reading Donald Goines and Iceberg Slim's Pimp and seeing movies like The Mack. I used to enter my room, face the mirror, and rap these songs to myself, trying to live up to the image these rappers gave off with their lyrics. Those who know me frequently remark on how excellent my lip synching is. However, it's easy to sing other people's lyrics; it's difficult to write your own. My feelings for Veronica were as gentle as terry cloth. I didn't have enough cold. The greatest reality, though, was that I was more interested in being liked than in being a player. And because I wasn't aiming for just any chick—I was aiming for the tens—I would typically get shot down. You would miss 100% of the shots you don't take, so I would shoot at a grown-up lady.

You never left the crib without a pen in the early nineties. A pen ensured that chance meetings lasted more than a few minutes, and you never knew who you would run into. This is from back when I used to wear New Balance sneakers with pen-pocket Polo, Guess, or Girbaud jeans. Although I can't recall what I said to make Veronica laugh, I do know that it caused her to laugh so hard that I had to use my pen to write down my phone number.

Before you knew it, we were always talking on the phone. The problem is that we would converse on the phone until we passed out, going by the moniker Ronnie. She was simply hanging out with me, so she was riding the bus down to the neighbourhood. We were in the park, holding hands while sitting on the steps, all that soft shit. We argued one day, and I recall being more like Iceberg Slim than I actually am.

"You have wounded my sentiments. I'm going," she declared.

She then walked away. I was acting cool on the outside, but inside I felt sick. Initially, I went inside the house and waited to contact her for the twenty minutes it would take her to return home. I called again and again to see if she had entered the house, but no one else answered. The phone rang and rang. It was at that moment that I heard the line, "Must be a bad connection, I give her my love and affection," from New Edition's song "Mr. Telephone Man." Finally, after what seemed like an hour, Ronnie responded.

"What do you desire?"

"Will you please please come back?"

Not at all. My feelings were damaged by you.

At that point in my life, I had never seen someone who was so aware of their emotions and thought highly of themselves enough to stand up for themselves. The majority of us were too preoccupied to see our emotions as assets, therefore we never bothered to learn how to comprehend them. Ronnie was standing there telling me that I had hurt something that I didn't even think I was capable of. I broke down in tears over the phone.

"I made a mistake. Don't leave me, please!

I sobbed like Tre from Boyz n the Hood for five minutes before she boarded the bus again. On my basement couch, we curled up and hugged each other. That's how my virginity ended. But Ronnie was the one who taught me a prerequisite—"You got to lick it before you stick it"—before I did.

That evening, I signed up. We had a rough relationship, but in 1994 I was locked up again at Vision Quest for something. However, I continued to stay in touch with her and phone her during my whole stay up there. After I assured her that I would be home shortly, they struck me with a 12-month sentence. I thought to myself, small things to a behemoth. I wrote her a letter once or twice a week. I never received mail back from Vision Quest over that entire year. I believed that someone in her house was hateful the entire time. The first person my friend drove me to see after I got out in the summer of 1995 was Ronnie.

I knocked on her door when we arrived in Uptown, and she answered.

"Boy, that gal. What's going on, really?

She steps outside into the heat, but her warmth disappears.

"Hi, what's going on?"

"I wrote you all those letters, damn you girl." Have you received them?

"Yes, I do have them."

That moment made me think of Martin from Blue Streak, the scene where he goes to see his girl and she gives him a curtsy after he wins the jail bid for the stolen diamond. Don't treat me this way! However, I remained composed. or made an attempt.

"Man, what have you been up to?"

She urged me to "come on." "Let's stroll along the road."

Thus, we strolled along the road. I kept telling her how beautiful she looked and giving her compliments the entire time. She tried her hardest to look happy. Looking back, it was obvious what was going to happen, but my vision was clouded by what I didn't want to see. She dropped a bomb on me as soon as we arrived at the block's corner.

"I found a man."

"What?"

My heart stopped at that very instant. There, I wanted to cry. However, I was too much of a player back then to know that I was playing myself.

CHAPTER 4
WELCOME TO THE JUNGLE

I heard someone say, "LOOK AT THIS SKINNY, BROKE motherfucker," as I was walking up the block, bored and trying to find something to occupy my time. The season was summer 1996. I turned to see Lil Shooter and Baby D, the two neighbourhood outcasts, running towards me. With haste, Lil Shooter took his hands out of his pockets, gripped his right hand with his left, and aimed his fingers like a pistol straight in my face. Twice he withdrew his trigger finger and narrowed his sinister hazel eyes. "Hi, nigga, welcome back to the block."

It was hard to give and receive hugs and kisses. Nor were "shit," "daps," or "pounds" the first salutations chosen. A volley of hooks and jabs from amateur shadowboxers is more welcome than a fucking high five. Big dogs like us were hardened and difficult to pet.

A few years older than me, Lil Shooter and Baby D were always linked at the hip. Seldom did you come across one without the other. They competed to see who could outdo the other, getting worse and worse in the process. Little Shooter has the build of a ninja in the martial arts. His body frightened me even as a young teen. He had thick shoulders, a narrow waist that resembled an inverted triangle, and strong, thick legs. Bruce Lee would be the father of the child you would anticipate Flo Jo and Bruce Lee to have. He could probably kick a hole through a brick wall if he so desired, but instead he used those horse hams to gallop down and drop the niggas before they had a chance to react. Most guys in the hood concentrated on performing pull-ups, push-ups, and sit-ups on monkey bars. Perhaps a few would occasionally lift weights, but from the waist down, they were often slender as fuck and stood on two sticks, making them extremely vulnerable to being struck by a Shooter through the concrete, regardless of how fast they could move.

The only thing that separated Baby D and Little Shooter was that one spot. Baby D was a small, fat fucker. He deliberately kept himself round, plump and heavy, so that he would have a reason to draw his rifle and fire from across the block. It appeared that they enjoyed hurting as many people as possible more than actually obtaining the money. The majority of people would advise avoiding them at all costs. However, it was wise of me to remain in those two wolves' good graces and keep them as close to me as possible at that time. It was best to have a group of cruel knuckleheads on the same side of the fence in my line of work, robbing, boosting, and stealing anything I could get my hands on, because otherwise, they would have made dinner out of me as well.

Hey! Hey guys, how are you? How are you doing?

It's not nothing. We just got back from using some hoes to kick it in the ditches," Baby D remarked.

"Man, get over your fat ass, nigga." "Those hordes weren't considering your ugly ass," Lil Shooter chuckled. Yes, they were having an affair with me until your dirty ass showed up! They simply don't want your crazy ass to steal their purse and pussy. Everyone laughed. The three of us headed up the street without exchanging plans. It seems as though there was an unwritten rule that said that if you found something to do when you had nothing else to do, someone would definitely get robbed—ideally not too soon.

I have to take the initiative in this. I had to move quickly and smoothly to avoid a sudden and dire turn of events. The best scenario was to find someone who would be easy to take advantage of and not put up much of a fight. Lil Shooter saw some of the chicks they were kicking it with earlier as we strolled up the roadway damaged by the crack.

"There they go, the hoes."

I gave Baby D a sidelong glance of mistrust.

"No, not them," Shooter looked crazy, though. And we did the same.

My rule was to never hurt anyone unless absolutely necessary, and I was the youngest, fastest, and only person who followed it. In order to steal the girls' earrings when they least expected it, I sprinted a little distance past them and lunged in their way on my own. However, things didn't quite turn out that way. Sheila, an older female I've always had my eye on, was one of the gals. As soon as I got my paper up and a little older, I vowed to make her mine. But before I could even run across the street to reach them, Sheila shocked me and asked, "Little Wally, where are you going?"

"Minimal?" I stopped and gave her the expression that suggested she had just split in my face. However, I was pressed for time because

Lil Shooter was only a few steps away, and I would much rather have a chain and a purse than have Shooter ruin her attractive appearance.

"Minimal?" With a quick flick of my right eye, I asked again. I pulled her necklace from her neck, her pocketbook, and the shopping bags from her partner with a growl, saying, "Gimme this little chain then, bitch." I launched myself, dragging my posterior back towards the men so they could reorient and abandon the females in their bewilderment. You would have thought Lil Shooter was attempting to get us all caught by the po-po because of how loudly he was laughing and shouting with amusement. When we halted, Baby D didn't say much; he simply gave me a damning look. You realise you made a mistake?

A used plastic bag hung off the door handle of a dilapidated liquor store where we set up shop. I took hold of it, packed it full of chains and handbags, and jammed it between Lil Shooter's ribs. I murmured, gasping for air, "Here." He gave me a disgusted expression.

He questioned, "Fuck you giving me this for?" "Oh my goodness, you pussy! Have you, young ass, previously heard about these hoes? I believed your build to be distinct. You behave exactly like this thug over here, a tender-dick. I could feel the tension building between them as he turned to face Baby D.

After running into Shooter, Baby D exclaimed, "Watch out, man," and turned to leave.

Yes, it's cool, I said. I hit those come-ups all day long every day; in addition, your dusty ass has to go purchase you some new shoes or whatever else. Along with your stank ass. I chuckled and threw away my cards, heading in the opposite direction.

Though I could feel his gaze glaring at me behind my eyes, I continued to walk nearly blindly, asking myself, "What the fuck did you just do, nut-ass nigga?" I knew that robbing the females would not work out well! They had more thurl brothers than not enough, and they were the itals. Even though the majority of them were Muslims, it didn't always matter how they handled their family business. Most of them became Muslims while incarcerated or when their fathers or uncles returned from serving a sentence and brought the discipline back to their homes. These men would go from being your least favourite adversary to your most feared ahki, the Arabic word for "brother." You didn't want to screw with them, I assure you. I have a good number of Muslim cousins as well, so I always thought I could pull myself out of a tight spot. However, I had no desire to initiate a fight of this nature anytime soon. Even as a small child, I knew that neighbourhood conflicts ought to be avoided wherever feasible.

I returned to my mother Jackie's place that evening. I was staying at Nanny's house when I wasn't at my mother's place, and I couldn't handle the idea of ahkis and their coming to visit me. It just felt sensible and best to go to my mother's house instead. Besides, even if everything did take off, Jackie most likely wouldn't be home. I was alone most of the time and could go wherever I pleased. I realised at this point that it would be simpler to avoid having to respond to inquiries about why I would continue to look out the window. I wished quietly that Hip, my stepfather, would stop by our home. We were able to communicate without using words in certain situations. He could read me like a book because he was from the streets. He would just start dropping jewels on how to go around at random; he wouldn't probe or try to take the juice out of me. He was never into the stick-up kid thing. It just wasn't his thing, and he thought it was unneeded. He was a member of the Center City Hustlers, a well-respected group that was also untouchable. "A robbery ain't nothing but a murder waiting to happen," was his assessment.

The neighbourhood junkies would start that begging nonsense as soon as I got to my block. "Yes, sir, do you have a little something for me?" I was starting to get paranoid about everyone. People used to send drug friends over to divert your attention and make you concentrate on their trembling hands counting out your dollars back then. Then, all of a sudden, you're getting popped on the sly because you're too busy staring at a dollar to see who or what else is around you.

"Dude, go somewhere and get the fuck on," I gritted my teeth. I was careful not to break any major patterns in what was thought to be a normal sequence of occurrences, but I was also firm enough that the dust head would know to return later at the very least.

I was mentally unwell. I remember being especially nervous about this final route. Stealing from someone I liked and knew was uncharted ground for me. My stomach continued to twist in knots, and every sound or shadow I went by seemed to pose a serious threat. I was taken aback to see my mother waiting for me at the door when I arrived home. With steely eyes and a knowing yet severe stance, she opened the door and gave me a thorough examination.

"What the hell is wrong with you, boy?"

"What's the matter with you?" I responded with a sultry tone. After chuckling, she put on her red-and-black leather jacket and walked out the door. She turned back and yelled, "Don't let anybody in my goddamned house, you hear me?" before shutting it. And for a split second, all I wanted was for her to stay with me.

A house party was where I was three weeks later. The closest you could get to flying high back then was during house parties, where rooms were filled with dense smoke from joints mixed with a dash of coke. You were going to end up a kite for the night whether you were smoking the shit yourself or just hanging around. The secondhand high was fun, even if I didn't trust it enough to engage in it as a group activity. I enjoyed how everything seemed to be mentally slowing down. My overactive mind was constantly at full capacity. What I liked best was the pleasant change in pace. Off that stank shake-and-bake smoke, I felt like a UFO.

"Are you going to hit the J, or are you just going to stand there looking silly?" I heard a feminine voice utter. It was fine-ass when I looked up to see who it was and who they were speaking to. Michelle was passing me a marijuana while she stood there with her girlfriends.

"Nope, I'm fine. "I'm already as high as the sky," I murmured, making my eyes appear downcast as though they truly were. They all chuckled together. Oh sh*t, I might have already left. So that these hoes don't think I'm bitch made, I might as well hit it. Yes, screw that and let me whack that.

"What did you hit?" Michelle replied angrily. "Little boy, even if I put this right under your nose, you wouldn't know what to do." I recognized then that she was experiencing the same thing as me and that we had moved past the topic of marijuana.

With haste, I said, "Let me hit it and find out."

There were folks from all around the way crammed into the kitchen, living room, and hallway. There were also some faces that were unfamiliar. You have to realise that I was younger than most of the folks there by at least seven or ten years. To be honest, the only reason I was able to get through was because I was not only Steven's crazy younger brother but also a hard worker who kept my mouth shut when the police arrived. The people in my area of work were looked down upon since we were likely to steal from the drug dealers of the day, who usually received the greatest accolades. But because I distributed the riches, I was unique.

Michelle yelled, "Wally," from the back room. My heart began to race. I licked the ash from around my lips and hastily smoothed down my T-shirt with my hands as I made my way through the throng of killers, dealers, and pimps. Michelle's thighs were directly behind the shiny chocolate calves of another woman's legs, which I could see as I drew nearer. Like a hound licking over a platter of leftover food, my mouth moistened. "Wally, I take it you've met my girlfriend before?"

She exclaimed, "You know, sexy-ass Sheila!" before I could refuse. Sheila straightened her back and looked directly at me.

Sheila said, "Hey Wally, thank you, boo," which completely baffled me.

With her perfectly styled hair, Michelle cocked her head. It's fantastic that you guys have met; this should be enjoyable!

I was in too much shock to talk.

Sheila looked across at Michelle. Yes, the day I told you these dirtballs robbed us on the street, Wally sent my stuff back in a janky-ass plastic bag with Baby D. His ass wasn't that dumb, I knew it! She giggled and gave Michelle a high five.

"Talk about the fucking devil," a voice at the doorway behind me exclaimed. It was Baby D and Little Shooter approaching me.

With a slow shake of her head and a finger to her lips, Sheila looked up and said, "Shhhh, don't say nothing!" There could not have been a more perfect timing.

Lil Shooter pulled the imagined trigger twice as he always did and yelled, "What up, soft-ass nigga," shoving his fingers into the side of my skull.

"Hey, family," I answered.

It's not nothing. We're going to blast this thing off and start doing something. Are you having fun?

Without hesitation, I nodded and started to leave through the doorway.

"Oh my god, sh*t. That's a yo bitch right there, Baby D. Stupid, big-headed Sheila? said the shooter. All five of our heads could be turned. We looked at each other for a moment, trying to process what was happening.

Baby D said, "Nah, man, she's cool," with a sly smile and a hint of laughter. We are not that way.

Little Shooter burst out laughing. "I thought that, you fat-ass nigga." With each step outside the room, we released the tension while laughing together and keeping the activity going.

The rain that we had missed while inside the celebration had left the streets damp. I wish I could have stayed at that party, damn you! There wasn't much movement and it was dead. Either everyone was hiding from the oppressively hot Philly heat somewhere, or they were at a house party getting some ass, like I was supposed to be. In any case, there wasn't much of anything to do. I made the call.

"Aye, yo, I'm leaving. I'll talk to you later.

Lil Shooter again aimed his fingers at my head while Baby D gave me a pound and nodded in accord.

"Pop-Pop," he murmured. Then he chuckled and grinned. "Aight, wager."

The ghastly duo bolted in the opposite direction as I hurried toward Jackie's house. Our natural thought process was to get in and out of the streets as fast as a bank robber. As I was getting closer, I could hear Little Shooter yelling. "What are you doing, Ah? How are you doing? Turning around, I saw Baby D shoving a gun into Lil Shooter's head, causing blood to pour from his head. I took off running.

That's when I discovered that power, money, and pussy can make even your best buddy turn into your worst enemy. Shooter had to learn this cruel lesson the hard way—I suppose Sheila was Baby D's "bitch"—through the process of self-discovery.

CHAPTER 5
SIX PIECE

The right side of my face began to twitch as usual before I could even round the corner into the parking lot of the chicken place that was located just around the block from Nanny's house. Every time I was travelling, I would get a not-so-subtle reminder to quicken my speed and take care of whatever needed to be done. I try not to look suspect as I jog lightly around the back of the restaurant, holding my gun securely in my sweaty palm and tucking it halfway into my hoodie pocket.

Hip attempted to teach me that once firearms are involved, there's no going back and everything will change as soon as he saw I was pursuing my passion. It modifies not just who you are but also the playing field.

I was mostly in agreement with him. Besides, I didn't have it in me to shoot anyone. I was by no means a tough guy, and I most definitely wasn't created that way—to shoot or kill someone? Never do that! Hip made sure I understood that life is irreversibly lost once it is taken, but basic items like money, clothes, and other material possessions can always be replaced. And my travels were going well without a gun until that moment. However, I went on an incredible journey with my original mentor, Big-Poppi, and he introduced me to a whole new method of making money.

At this point, Big-Poppi was far ahead in the heist. I was still researching faster ways to get compensated outside of boosting at this point. It went okay when we went shopping. While I was working, it took too long for me to hit the racks, open the bags, and sell whatever I could. Everything was moving too slowly. "I wouldn't dare risk it all just to profit off scraps," the original poster said. And that's when he took the gat out of his pocket. He explained to me how much simpler life may be when one is carrying a piece. He pulled the car over at Twenty-Second and Indiana, between the Video Shack and the bank, telling me he could show me better than tell me.

OG didn't speak all that much. He may not have even given me instructions. We both jumped out of the car as the money manager was making his morning deposit, and he immediately handed me the revolver.

"Go to it; you are aware of what this is. Make it quickly and empty the damned bag!" Big-Poppi bellowed. The fact that there were neither arguments nor queries startled me. I had never seen an armed robbery go as smoothly as a warm knife cutting through a bean pie before in my brief career as a crook.

I never created fifteen stacks that easily before. It was unbelievable to me. I nearly felt foolish for taking so much time, abiding by the law in an attempt to uphold some semblance of morality, and robbing without using handguns to keep the area orderly. This motherfucker, on the other hand, just took five minutes, without breaking a sweat, to make what I would take a week to make. I was exhausted and out of breath as I sat in the car, my heart still beating; by the time we got to the next block, I had already decided to screw that! I have to get myself a bit!

When I got back home, my head was still reeling from what I had just done, so I circled around. I couldn't wait to do that same crap on my own. I had never owned a pistol before this day, but I was now determined to get one first thing in the morning.

It didn't take me more than twenty-four hours after obtaining a gun to start going door-to-door at least twice a week in quest of a new play. I kept hearing Hip's words in the back of my mind: "Do your thing, but leave those guns alone." Everyone's life can end with one bad decision. I was troubled by those statements nearly every day. The excitement of gaining even more power, however, was too great for the ghosts of failed thefts to catch up with. Packing heat gave off an authority that was really powerful. It was more about getting away with it quickly and swiftly and moving closer to leaving my situation than it was about the thought of subduing another person.

I didn't want to live a life of crime, but that's all I knew. Busting routes prevented my family and I from going without while friends and neighbours went to bed hungry or with holes in their shoes. Nonetheless, I sometimes felt empty and lost inside of me. I was aware that my life embodied the epitome of identity theft.

A garbage can was holding the rear door slightly open as an early-morning KFC employee prepared for the day, just as was to be expected. In order to prevent anyone driving from behind the restaurant from seeing what I was doing, I ran up to the drive-thru window and placed my body against the frame.

"Ohh... good morning," she uttered in a perplexed and nervous tone. "You have to go around through the front door, baby, and not back here." And with that, I slid through the broken door and aimed a nickel-plated.22 handgun at her ribcage, cutting her off before she could continue her statement.

"Look, lady, just give me the fucking money and I'll get on with it, don't trip over it." The twitch of nerves tugged at my lip and right eye, giving me the impression of a growling savage dog. I saw the safe hidden behind the counter on the other side of the greasy kitchen floor as I yelled at her to stop hesitating and give up the money from the register that wasn't hers. I signalled angrily for her to open it by getting down on the ground. My stomach turned over with frustration at her hesitancy. Every second counted, and I would have to create a more violent character the longer it took. "Get moving, bitch, before you force me to harm you!" However, everybody who knows me understands that I could never force myself to be aggressive or shoot someone. Oddly enough, unlike everyone else who broke into these institutions, I never once gave mask wear any thought. I wanted other people to have the impression that I was just a kind guy doing a bad thing. If you could see me, you could feel me, I thought. Since that seemed to be the reality to me. Furthermore, this isn't even your cash. This is not a personal attack. Who will it actually hurt, anyway? That was how I thought. Even as it started to get emotionally taxing, I was still able to pull off these capers because of that rhetorical question.

I distinctly recall feeling a specific way when I woke up that chilly fall October morning in 1996. There was something there, like a gut feeling I couldn't quite place, but nothing particularly stuck out from any other Monday. I remember being thoughtful at the age of seventeen and a half, wondering if rapping with my favourite older cousin, Gillie, would be a better route to the nicer things I was risking my life for.

Gillie and I had only been together for a year, despite the fact that we were cousins. One day, when these boys were rhyming in a cipher, I was returning home from one of my childish moments when I noticed Gil standing right there. In casual gatherings called "ciphers," people would spit out their hottest bars. During my teenage years, I had a strong belief that I would become a rapper and would often rhyme. The rappers with the better bars continued as the cipher went on, and the others just watched. That's what transpired between Gil and me. Gil and I were the final two standing after a few revolutions. When we start fighting, Gil bodies me. Watching the crowd's reaction during a conflict tells you so much about it, and it becomes clear when to concede.

I told Girl he was polite after the fight and asked for his number because I could relate to Dice Raw, a well-known Philadelphia rapper who was at the time having sex with the Roots. This coincided with the release of their album Do You Want More?!!!??!. After a span of two days, I call Gil and instruct him to visit Nanny's crib. He approached the crib, and upon seeing him, Stevie exclaimed, "Cousin, what's up?" My cousin? I guess Stevie noticed my bewildered expression and clarified that we were linked as cousins on his father's side by our grandmothers. I realise that some of you are scratching your heads and wondering how Wallo could not know his cousin. Even though you all reside in the same city, there's a chance that I missed some of the most significant aspects of your lives in the chaos of my constant ripping and running.

I remember sitting on the side of my bed in October 1996, holding a knot of hundreds that was secured with rubber bands. I nodded my head while quoting Ice-T's "High Rollers" rap, treating it as if it were the Ten Commandments: "Extreme cash flow, extreme dress code, vulgar vocabulary, definition: street player, you know who I mean." I fell asleep, daydreaming about what it would be like to be a member of a rap group, doing our thing. Yes, that would be everything—me and Gil crushing it on stage, going on tour, and snatching up all the baddest hoes!

Music is God to me, or perhaps God is a DJ. At that age, music was the solution to everything. I always relied to music to get me through difficult times, whether they were related to love, breaking up with a girl, or just trying to ignore the poor weather. To be really honest, a lot of my most rash and impetuous decisions have been guided by the lyrics from some of my favourite bands. It had a way of turning the real world into a motion picture. It was my brutal reality's score. I was a half-baked danger before music turned me into a true street devil. Ice-T was my theme music that day, and I started having dreams about Gillie's and my own songs.

I reached for the rucksack lying on the ground beside me, hoping to find a pen so I could start composing a few bars, but then I stopped and said to myself, Man, who are you fooling? For the past two academic years, this bag hasn't had a pen or notepad! I laughed so hard at myself that I thought I may wake someone else as I looked up and saw my reflection in the broken mirror on the dresser. I told myself, There go the big lights, the stardom, and all the groupie hoes. My fictitious rap group with my cuzzo swiftly went dark because I stole anything that wasn't a pen and/or pad out of my rucksack.

My lucky charm was the black hooded hoodie I had on that morning. It smelled awful and had a ton of ugly ketchup stains, but that was the kind of grime that came with the job. The stick-up kid's uniform was a sweatsuit and hoodie, regardless of how much name-brand fly junk I had stacked up in my wardrobe. Like stripes on a soldier's sleeve, I proudly wore it. To put it bluntly, I couldn't care less what was on that jawn; I was not going to remove any of that fortunate charm from it.

The weeks that before that day had been incredibly delightful. I completed a couple smooth, successful routes without any problems at all. I used to be really confident and blatantly proud of myself; I had gone from learning the ins and outs of the business from Steve to blasting routes on my own like a well-tuned machine. After removing my "how to rob a motherfucker" training wheels, I quickly went from being "Steve's little brother" to just "Wallo."

Steven, my elder brother who was smaller in stature, was an expert in anything he set his mind to. Despite being five years older than me, his movements gave the impression that he had defeated me by a lifetime. He was as passionate about the hustler's life as Steve's father, Pop, and my father, Wallace. When it came to obtaining money and making sure he looked presentable while doing it, Little Steve didn't play around. Steve stood out from the crowd due to his caramel-coloured skin and curly hair, resembling that of a Puerto Rican. We called him "Little Steve" because of his little stature. However, his energy and aura were far more magnificent than any grown man I had ever seen playing hustler. I aspired to have his level of ease. His cunning was unrivalled, flawless, and unfucking obvious. He may be standing in front of you talking, snatching your wallet out of your coat pocket, taking out your credit card, and then putting it back in.

My motto was, "Just a few more routes, and I'll be done."

I knew that as soon as I walked into the filthy chicken kitchen that October day, I had to get rid of every idea that didn't align with my purpose. I couldn't make decisions with both feet in and out of the picture. I was using my anxious twitch to lend me frightening facial expressions when I noticed a police car approaching slowly from the corner of my eye.

I mentally mapped out my next move, terrified, but telling myself to be calm, Wallo.

The officer questioned, "Ma'am, is everything okay?" with suspicion.

"Hello, yes, everything is fine." Concealing the revolver in my right hand, I waved him off with my empty left, confirming.

The policeman parked and circled the drive-through, but something told me he was simply phoning for backup and would return. I snuck passed the agitated woman, who was now shouting because she was upset that I was late for the money grab. I stepped out the side door and slipped over the slick floor. Wee, ooh, wee, ooh, wee. In the near distance, the noises of at least three or four police cars driving across the main intersection could be heard.

With my heart racing at a thousand beats per minute, I turned abruptly to the left and started sprinting across the block. More police cars were racing toward me, blowing through red lights at high speed. I pulled out the revolver, threw it beneath a parked car, spun around, and began dragging people toward Broad Street and Clearfield.

I was about to give up when I noticed Mr. Sammy, the father of a boyhood buddy, walking a few blocks ahead. Mr. Sammy was a highly esteemed member of the community. He was yelling at me to come toward him and waving me down. Terrified and running for my life, I prayed that Mr. Sammy wouldn't catch me.

"Listen to me, Wallo," he murmured as he grabbed me and wrapped his arms around me. I'm not sure what you did, but follow my instructions so that I can help you get through this securely.

I was fatigued, so my automatic response was to say, "Fuck that," and keep running. My spirit, mind, and body were all worn out. Tears filled my eyes as I fell face down into the ground. Even though Nanny's house was still only a few blocks away, I would have done anything to go back in time and spend that time with her, going through old photo albums with my dad inside.

CHAPTER 6
INTERROGATION

Whether I wanted it to or not, being in that stale, dark, and dusty interrogation room had my mind wander down memory lane. I was upset. I went over all of my mistakes and left turns that I should have taken right back. Like a page out of a life storybook, mistakes and treasured memories flashed before my eyes. I kept asking myself why I had made the choices I had and why it was so hard for me to just accept that I had made them. Why didn't I just complete my education and move on? I tried so hard not to think about the possibility that I would be certified and tried as an adult this time, but all those memories came flooding back to me.

Anyone with half a functioning brain would assume that after five years going back and forth in juvenile correctional facilities, I would have learned my lesson. I made an effort. Despite having a longer hooky record than the books my teachers were making me read, I started attending school and attending a few lessons. It had been nearly two years since my last stay in the correctional facility, but I was making the effort to do the right thing. With the greatest of intentions, I was in route to becoming an even greater student, friend, son, and young man. I vowed to God that I would get my act together and avoid anything that was causing the problems I was always having. I was going to take a different route.

The court counsellor pressed, "Mr. Peeples, isn't it true that if it weren't for Mr. Sammy protecting you from your own stupidity, you probably wouldn't be sitting here in this courtroom?" "There was a very real chance that you would be shot and killed by the police, who, incidentally, were just doing their duty and might have taken your life or, heaven forbid, someone else's. Can you imagine how much worse things may have gotten? You alone would have been the one to bear the consequences for that! That's correct, Mr. Peeples. As she twirled on her tired, block-stacked heels, her words faded away. I wasn't sure if she was really trying to trick me with these protracted inquiries or if she was just trying to shake me for some reason, since if it was the latter, it seemed to be working.

I scanned the courtroom, expecting to meet the gaze of a caring eye, someone who would give me a "I get you" look. Everything will work out OK. However, I saw that even my mother and Nanny had lost trust in the system and in me. My family had had enough of the burden I had placed on them and my failed promises. They had this strange feeling that if I was imprisoned for a long enough period of time, something would eventually change and I would emerge a different person. However, I had to fight for my rehabilitation before I could see any real results, and that didn't happen until I lost patience with myself.

THE COURTROOM GOT QUIET, AND THE ONLY THING I COULD HEAR WAS THE WALL Clock's second hand ticking away. The next thing I knew, I was outside being led back to the tombs while still wearing handcuffs. I yanked my arms away from what we used to call "toy cop courtroom security" and cried, "Yo, let me go." I had no idea where I was at all.

The officer grinned ugly across his mug and added, "Yo punk ass got a ten to twenty max, and I could make that time real fucked up for you if you don't relax."

"Ten to twenty at most?" I asked myself again. What is ten to twenty?

"Years."

Two correctional officers stormed into my holding cell, banging a couple of hefty brown backpacks filled with cuffs and steel chains. The sacks included ankle and wrist restraints for my transportation to SCI Dallas. I had never before been cuffed. Yes, they were handcuffed, but never in chain-gang fashion! I attempted to cling to the few minutes I still had in this world that I had already come to know. The sound of those chains clattering together became too loud to ignore, and I found myself on the verge of losing my friends, family, and freedom. The noise became closer and louder the harder I attempted to ignore what was about to happen, signalling to me that my life as I knew it was coming to an end.

"People," exclaimed the short, stout C.O. I remained silent and did not bother to respond. They didn't need my help to strap me up for the bus voyage to hell because they knew where I was.

The thick metal door behind us banged loudly. Twelve of us offenders were prepared to be sent away. Suddenly, I started to recall various Bible stories, like the one about the twelve disciples and the breaking of bread. All I know is that, during that particular incident, with each stride our chain gang took together, the church appeared to be the only place my thoughts would wander. However, I clung to the vision, almost going blindly.

"Sweetheart, wake up! You're no longer in juvie camp," the other chubby correctional officer teased.

I said, "No shit," hoping against hope that anyone would hear.

On the two-hour bus ride to the state prison, the majority of us kept to ourselves. Some people talked a lot of stuff, cursed a lot, and made a lot of outrageous threats. When I turned to face the person who was tripping the most, I saw that his ankles and wrists were covered in black boxes. Though I was ignorant of its meaning, I deduced that it implied the motherfucker was unfit for play. Later on, I discovered that the black boxes served as an extra line of defence for some of the worst motherfuckers to be imprisoned—the blatant killers who really had no fear of anybody. I instantly averted my gaze. I made an effort to shift my concentration and have a last look at the world I was leaving behind via the window grilles. I still couldn't figure out where I was or where I was heading, though, because of the grating and the salty tears that began to well up in my eyes.

Every cell block was outside in the yard at the same time as our bus arrived, right in time for recreation hour. Hundreds of burly men, ripped and bruised like UFC fighters, were present. A two-hour trip from North Philadelphia is required to get to SCI Dallas, a state prison located in Luzerne County, Pennsylvania. About 2,000 criminally condemned individuals reside there, 400 of them are serving life sentences. Consider this: Two out of every ten inmates you came across there were never going home. They were home, as far as the state was concerned. However, I was surrounded by men who were aware of their last resting place.

And here I was, seventeen years old and tiny, going to be put in a cage with big, bad men! Oh no, sh*t! How the hell did I get into this? I became frightened. When I visited my stepfather and uncle up here, there was a big change in what I witnessed from my first prison experience. When I visited, I would head straight to the visiting room, get some snacks from the vending machine, play cards, engage in some grease talk, and occasionally I would run with twenty or more other prisoners in one area. However, I was genuinely terrified when I saw the prison yard from this angle. As I vividly saw myself being mercilessly trampled, I realised I needed to locate something, or someone, to defend me right now.

The cells they placed me in were about the size of an eight by ten room—a bathroom in a house. The air was heavy with the sickening smell of dirty ass, crusty toe-jammed feet, and god knows what else. The floors were slimy, chilly, and damp. I'm not sure what else could be the devil's playground if this one! In your bathroom, everything that you do happens. There isn't a kitchen, living room, bathroom, or any of that. There is no driveway and no basement. For years, the two of them shared that place. You live there. And my cellmate has to take it when I mention that we're living in the bathroom. I'm sitting at the table two feet away as he poops and covers that joint with the cabinet in the bed. He's only going to play the mean flush game, which will minimise the scent because in jail you have the power flush, which makes you flush continuously.

I've tried to come up with another way to describe what it's like to live in a cell, but the reality is that I'm so institutionalised that I just consider it normal. You have to adjust your perspective on things while incarcerated. It's the sole means of surviving. If I had considered events from the perspective of what was happening outside the wall, I would have lost my mind from fear. You're in trouble when you're shaken. Furthermore, the time you do start to mess with you when you're in difficulties.

From the time the bus arrived, with all of us strapped together, I knew that I wouldn't be staying longer than necessary. I realised that in order to put my life back on the correct track, even if I didn't fully grasp what my purpose was. As a scared adolescent pulling up to the yard, I had no idea that I would soon start transforming my life. I was the one who encouraged everyone who would listen to improve on their performance even by one small item every day. My new moniker, "the Happiest Nigga in Prison," came to pass at that point. And since I had no intention of earning stripes from an institution that offered nothing more, I was fine with that.

But it took me some time to arrive.

During my first two weeks at SCI Dallas, everything seemed unreal. It felt a little bit like a neighbourhood reunion at times since I ran into so many old bunkies from all the years I'd spent in juvenile detention and friends from around the route.

You could always hear "Aye, yo Wallo" coming from the other side of the yard whenever I went outside. If we were lucky, we might have been able to check in and take each other's temperatures through the fence for a short while.

"Yeah, Slim, this motherfucker gave me life, but that's not all for naught." I'll be returning home in a moment after being released from appeal. I could have paid for a renowned mob lawyer to get me out of there before my time if I had a $1 for each time I heard that same line! It was insane; I saw friends from all over the neighbourhood up there, and it was kind of comforting to know that I had a few kind people in case I needed to make a move. The only difference was that, although officially recognized as adults, my young allies and I remained apart from the older men until we turned eighteen. It seemed as though they were eager to remove the training wheels before releasing us from the bubble to face the real wolves on our own.

The majority of the prisoners were from Pittsburgh, North and South Philadelphia, and the tiny villages that lay between. Based on sexual orientation, race, and city, territories were created. There were designated areas for gay men and women. In my opinion, some of the more effeminate-presenting males were ten times more aggressive with the knuckle game than straight guys, so I'm not sure if it was put in place to protect them from us or us from them. I swear, you had another thing coming if you ever thought you could get one over on them for being soft as shit. In addition, there was an unwritten rule that if you got into a fight with one of them, it would be taken for a lover's dispute and you would be looked upon suspiciously going forward. The key takeaway from the gate was to either mind your own fucking business or get ready to be worked. Regretfully, that lesson alone had more weight within the cage than all the verses combined from the Bible and the Quran combined. There are certain things that happened behind those walls that many would kill to see come to light; things that may destroy families, incite lethal rivalries, or worse, leave you feeling as though you've been split open to the white meat with no one there to support you. Even though I was naturally curious about everything and everyone, I was aware that many things I didn't know or comprehend shouldn't be questioned.

Months passed by steadily over the course of weeks, and before I knew it, I was turning eighteen. The elderly, white, wrinkled jail officer with pepper-and-salt hair hummed, "Happy birthday to you." He jiggled his keys to get me out of the dorm and his ass was as delighted as a pig in dung. On the route to my destination, a state guardsman hummed "Happy Birthday" to me when I woke up, which was unfortunate for me. "People, wake up." It's time for you to start growing hair on your chest, he declared with pride. I thought I could have been better off dead at that very time, which was my eighteenth birthday.

UPDATED, A convict from inside the registration office threw a bundle of blankets, a shirt, and prison pants directly at my head. I've never been the sportiest cat by any stretch of the imagination, but I was able to grab my new uniform and cell bedding just in time to avoid looking foolish by spilling them on the wet floor.

"Sinclair! The registration officer's raspy voice shouted, "Get the fuck out of here."

"What do I do, Mrs. Walker?" the prisoner in the brown outfit said, acting as though he was ignorant.

I blurted, "Whoa, whoa, whoa, nah, Mrs. Lady, I'm okay, he's cool," before she could respond.

With a giggle, Sinclair shot back at me, "Shut the fuck up, little nigga, and mind your business," and he left the office by walking down the corridor. This is a bitch, I thought to myself. I had hardly been in the adult penitentiary for an hour when I started to feel like a loser.

While some prisoners were waiting to be checked in, others were observing me closely like hawks. But even before I reached this point, where the actual big dogs were, I understood that I wasn't built for anything tough and that I needed to quickly become adept at this new land's mental warfare.

People. "Please enter and take a seat," the registration officer said. Mrs. Walker had dark eyes and was a Caucasian woman. I sat down, hoping that my innocent deer-in-headlights looks would win her over.

People, this is how you will always be identified. You are now prisoner DG2670. Should you be discovered anywhere without your identity, you will be placed in isolation. Are you able to comprehend me? With no intention of looking at me, she asked.

"Yes," I said, lowering my own.

"Oh, and this part right here is missing," she remarked, gesturing to a blank space on my prisoner's page. "In the event of your death, where would you like your body sent?"

She saw the horror on my face, realised I was still a minor, and rephrased it. Who should we call in the event of a medical emergency, according to you?

Very nothing was done to lessen the blow of reality by the reframing. This place might kill me. Nobody suspects they might be in a cell or a pine box when they're chasing the streets. I sobbed myself to sleep that night.

CHAPTER 7
COMING OF AGE

Man, if you don't get over this bullshit and get the fuck away from me. As I turned the corner to return to my cell, I heard my bunky, Mitch, yell at Ray. "I told y'all that boy was stupid." As the designated block messenger, Ray seemed to be someone Mitch didn't want to hear crap from.

There was a messenger assigned to each block, who served as a go-between for various cliques and crews, passing along messages and cautions. Usually, someone who has no business being in jail in the first place is assigned to this role, which is predetermined. They are typically the square bears of the real world, most likely connected to someone powerful behind closed doors, or perhaps they managed business for an outsider with enough clout to influence decisions behind closed doors. They were frequently accountants or other financial guys who helped big-time dealers launder money; as a result, they were charged with first-degree misdemeanours, or "M1," for the unrelated death of a body. In any case, they were usually too insignificant to be involved in any crews working on the blocks, but they were also too important to a head honcho to be screwed up like the other squares who were punched and mistreated for their commissary and other things.

When I arrived at our cell, Ray had already climbed back up the tier and was stuffing what appeared to be a few boxes of Newports into his jeans.

"Dog, what happened? Or what? Did you get knocked down for your ports? I inquired with Mitch. I was flying straight into my cell wall the next thing I knew.

"Kid, I'm telling you to stop playing so much and mind your own business. Stop it!"

With Mitch holding the back of my hurting head, I rose up from beneath the sink basin. "Dude, what did I do? Hold up."

"You talk way too much."

What topic was he discussing?

I never would have imagined that my bunky and I would be involved in it, but there I was, blocking and swinging in the first of several jail rumbles that I had no business being in. In that little room, we grappled with each other, squeezing one other by our stiff brown shirts and delivering powerful body punches. With every punch we delivered, we grated our teeth and cursed, "Fuck you, nigga," while doing our hardest not to make too much noise. We battled as gently as we could because we both knew that no matter what happened, neither of us wanted to be taken to "the hole," or solitary confinement.

Since Mitch was much stronger than I was and had undoubtedly thrown more hands before, it was really easy for him to beat my ass and end our altercation quickly. Curled up like a puffy cheese doodle between our bunk railing and the cinder block, I felt dazed. With his fists clenched like a set of bowling balls, Mitch gazed down at me, panting furiously. He spit right near my tucked-in, curled-up body.

Everything occurred so quickly; he threw me on the floor and then reached out to assist me up. He roared like a madman and said, "I could kill yo ass, young'n." I wish you could have seen the expression of bewilderment that spread across my whole grill. Though I hoped it wasn't another setup, I went out to touch his hand since I knew I didn't want any more smoke from him. "Straight up, if anyone asks you, let them know I handled my biz here with you," Mitch replied, pulling me to my feet. Do you hear me?

"Hold 'em. You are capable of that.

Gasping for air and pacing in four-by-four-foot circles, I took a few moments to think about Mitch's next move. Mitch took off the white T-shirt that was sagged at the collar. He just went about his business with precision and with the composure of a surgeon. I watched as he blew his trademark whistle, stepping onto the tier and beckoning the homies to gather in the dayroom once the guards had left their posts.

Whoosh. That noise represented the exhalation of breath leaving my lungs. It was sufficient to completely fill an air mattress in one sitting. I had no idea that I was holding my breath, waiting for Mitch to break free from the jail and leave me to fuck myself. My thoughts were a total haze. It was definitely a wake-up call, even if I had no understanding why what had transpired had happened. It didn't take a genius to figure out that, whatever the purpose of this beating, it was a method of discipline and character development used to prevent worse consequences. In that sense, the streets—and jail protocol in particular—are dysfunctional. An ass whoopin always appeared to be the initial course of action with any lesson you learnt, no matter how basic or harmful the scenario, even in moments of purported brotherly love or slum attempts at manly teaching.

Ray stopped directly in front of my cell doorway as I was gathering my courage to get ready for chow. The possibility that he was assigned to do the job made me curl my fist up. However, Ray chuckled. "Calm down, Slim. I'm just stopping by to give you the message."

I moaned, "Well, what the fuck is the message?"

He warily peered over his shoulder and stated, "No, the message isn't for you; I need to relay the message that you got dealt with the way you were supposed to."

But to whom should you deliver the word, Ray? And for what purpose? How the hell did I do this? I asked in a very worried manner.

"Slim, calm down; it's not that serious. You simply happened to catch your first infraction, but you could have gotten away with it far simpler."

"Infraction?" I asked again.

"Hey Slim, even in prison there's freedom in the world. You are free to do as you like and hang out with whomever you choose, but there are processes in place to ensure that things move well, so you have to know who, what, and when to speak up about specific issues. I listened intently and just gave a face of pure perplexity. Ray gave a long, heavy sigh. "Observe. There are rumors that you informed a Puerto Rican niggas about the high prices being paid for smokes and smut magazines on our side of the fence. That is the transgression! Ignoring your affairs revealed the additional points we were adding to everything. It somewhat screwed us over in the marketplace. You have to realise, Wallo, that in order for us to stay above the fray, we have to maintain a very complex network of the jail economy. This kind of mistake has the potential to ruin someone's life! You must learn to speak slowly and listen quickly.

I informed him who and where he could cop all the nice shit from, recalling that I had been shooting the shit with one of the new guys at the time. I just assumed I was watching out for everyone, sh*t. Mitch benefits financially from all of this while José gets his fill of nicotine and has fun with the Black Tail publications. In my opinion, that would be a win-win situation.

Slim, you're a small-time robber, not a hustler! You're fortunate to have your parents and a few allies here to watch out for you; otherwise, you would have been reprimanded severely for the trash you did, you understand? Wallo, this isn't a game. There's nothing cute or charming about the lives that half of these cats lead in the Palace. You're at the bottom of the hierarchy that exists here. Behind these gloomy walls, a thief is just a woman beater and a paedophile on a higher level. When it comes right down to it, Ray remarked firmly, "You never put in any real work; you're just a taker, and that doesn't give you no stripes as a man." That was the first time I considered it that way and experienced a sickening sense of humiliation.

"You look good, Ray," I nodded.

"Please don't thank me," he answered. "Please just move out of the way. Don't let your loose lips turn you into a booty bandit's dinner.

I resolved to behave as foolishly as possible after that. I used to talk about my time as if I knew nothing at all. I would act as if I was a frog in every situation from that point on, and nobody would ever ask me for anything or have any expectations of me. Please call me Kermit and don't touch my silly green ass.

ABOUT A YEAR OR TWO into my time in prison, I was in the yard one afternoon and I overheard this dispute between buls from different parts of Philly. One of them had a drug package in, and the other found out. As they were arguing, they walked into the area where the weightlifting equipment was held.

"Motherfucker, stop. I told you!"

The next thing I saw was the bull from South Philly falling over and the bull from North Philly bashing his skull in with a ten-pound weight with so much force that the blood shooting out of his head was like oil was struck—and what terrified me more was the fact that the bull from South Philly was still fighting, even with the blood loss. Though there were two guards on their post in the watchtowers, they were about 300 feet away. And while that's not a great amount of distance, by the time the guards intervened, the bull from North Philly had already hit South Philly ten or fifteen times. All of this transpired in a matter of minutes. For the two buls beefing, both of them had life sentences, so they were literally fighting for their lives.

Despite that incident, contrary to what many people may believe and how it's portrayed in television and movies, prison is one of the most respectful places I've ever been in my life. And I'm going to tell you why: because the smallest little thing could ignite a war, and tensions are so high, everyone prioritises their safety and survival. Especially when you know you have a life beyond the cell.

The tension and air in the chow hall were so thick that the only way to cut through it was with one of those antique turkey hand saws that rural people kept in their kitchen junk drawer. Of course, at the chow hall, there was always a chance to get shanked with a filed-down pipe or cracked overhead the head with a rock in a sock, and I was terrified that it would be my turn. To be really honest, I could honestly state that, unlike the majority of other young buls, I didn't always fear for my life until I made this dumbass mistake. Of course, there was always the possibility that some strange, unnatural deed would appear out of nowhere and threaten us with violent storms and mudslide clouds. I could have easily been a victim, especially when it came time to use the showers as a young kid. However, those were isolated incidents, and I made every effort to stay out of those precarious circumstances. Even if it meant occasionally forgoing a few days of baths and cleaning my feet and underarms in the cell sink while smelling like corn chips.

When I traversed the battlefield known as the chow hall, not a single eye failed to glance at me. I stopped to recall that the ass whip'n I had just received was essentially a consideration hall pass because they had let my own bunky to reprimand me for what, in my opinion, was still only a small mistake. When it came time for my performance, the males in the cafeteria were eager to give me the cold shoulder. My gait became somewhat erratic, I began to drag my left leg a little, and I tucked my tongue into the side of my cheek while holding my face with my hands to give the impression that I had my ass severely battered.

"People!" C.O. Cole was calling my name from across the cafeteria, and I jumped at the sound. One of the sickest, meanest guards in the place was this motherfucker. Not even the most seasoned killers had messed with him. We called him "Cold Blooded," but we said it in whispers only, never speaking the name aloud. Saying Candyman's name five times in front of the mirror was how it felt. It was so bad that you would know it was time to put yourself on voluntary time-out without asking questions, should somebody merely imply that Cold Blooded was on the prowl. This six-five ogre didn't give a damn, and one of his favourite pastimes was torturing you before writing you up to spend eighteen months or more in the pit. That was nothing compared to having his dick sucked by a peon who was terrified of being alone for long periods of time. He was insane, and calling me out in front of everyone was the first of his ridiculous mind games that he enjoyed playing for amusement with the rest of us inmates.

I almost felt a crick in my neck from whipping my head so quickly toward the enormous wildebeest that I almost forgot I was meant to be seriously hurt. My feet started to feel like they were drowning in quicksand as my body froze. There were only the two of us in that particular area of the chow hall, although there had to be at least fifty of us cons there. As everyone watched, Cold Blooded and I met gaze.

"Guy, what the fuck is wrong with you?" he exclaimed, slicing through the line of chow like Moses did the Red Sea.

It always amazed me how, at the most unlikely moments, a Bible tale from Sunday school would come to mind, such as when I was afraid I might be trampled or worse, die. That's probably one of the consequences of growing up with a so-called "prayer grandma," as there was nothing quite like picturing God showing up to save your stupid ass during uncertain times. There's no turning back from some bitch-ass crap like that, I swear. Had I not grabbed onto a powerful memory at that very moment, I would have fucked out like a drama queen.

C.O. Cole savagely shoved his billy club up against my face, ribs, thighs, and back, prodding around potential sensitive spots to see what hurt enough for me to admit to an earlier square-up. "I said to you, people, what the fuck happened to you?" This time, he scanned the chow hall for a guilty expression or glance, or even to check if anyone had any visible bruising or marks on their knuckles. When it came to him, the saying goes that nothing is better than being able to rough off at least two cons for the price of one.

I would have been called a snitch if I had simply blinked an eye incorrectly. Looking across the sea of grim-faced prisoners waiting for me to slip, I made the decision that I would rather be in the pit for the next eighteen months than be labelled as a cellblock thief who is now a snitch. I was going to have to choose between two poisons, and calling someone a rat was not an option. Fuck.

"Cold, calm down..." Before I called him our pet name, I realised what I was doing. "C.O. Cole, nothing happened at all. Really. I was dreaming about one of the baddest bitches in the city that I left alone, and I was just lying on my top bunk. Dick hard as a rocket, you know there was a party in my pocket. Then all of a sudden, as I was going to climb upon that warm, silky bitch, my stupid ass gave way from the top bunk with such force that it resembled a dope junkie being thrown from paradise. Cole, I fucked my entire shit up, real rap."

Just behind me, on the table, sat Mitch and a couple of his crew members, watching the whole thing come apart. I glanced over my shoulder to make sure they knew I held it down for the homies and to see if they heard me caving in to requests. Error #3. My initial thought was that I was Bob Barker from The Price Is Right. Making eye contact with the guys, who didn't even try to maintain their composure, came in third. The second was putting on a show for everyone on the block to witness. Mitch and the others at the table couldn't contain their laughter. That crap turned Cold Blooded smooth off, and before I knew it, my face was being introduced to C.O. Cole's elbow. Whoa!

Now, how in the world did I go from being pounded twice in one afternoon to leading a somewhat respectable life (in comparison to the nightmares of others) in one of the worst jails outside of Philadelphia? This is really ridiculous! I pondered in my mind. The best hand, though, was getting whooped by one man and put to the hole while everyone forgot about my transgression.

During my three years behind bars, I saw some of the most diligent men emerge from prison completely altered from when they entered. I'm speaking of males who were once beasts among men experiencing extraordinary physical and psychological transformations. You can permanently lose your marbles when you are in total isolation and the only sounds outside of your skull are the blood-curdling cries and the sound of men's skulls smashing against paint-chipped walls every night. The sound of men screaming incoherently from boxes a few steps away from you often inspires you to tell incredible stories in the pit. The only company you can have in this horrible location are the bedbugs, who will tear your flesh to pieces if you stay long enough to understand when to ignore them and when to enjoy their company.

Even yet, I still preferred the hole to the prospect of being called a rat—a transgression that no one will ever forget or forgive.

Cold Blooded got to work on me right away, yanking my still thin frame out of the cafeteria and throwing me into a holding cell—which was often reserved for those who had been classified as insane, or 5150. I could have sworn it made him even more violent and enraged, but you couldn't pay me to fight back, say smack, or show even the tiniest hint of resistance. He was asking for something from me that I was not ready to offer.

Apart from his intense liking for this kind of aggressive prison foreplay stuff, there was no reason for C.O. Cole is so excited. "Get off your ass, motherfucker! Your bare-naked ass and the lint from up under those little bitch-made balls are the only things I want to see, loser.

I yelled, "Whoa, whoa, whoa," considerably louder and more impolitely than I would have liked to have addressed him. However, I must defend myself by saying that, prior to the anxiety's muted chokehold taking hold of me, I was desperately fighting to regain control over my senses, making it hard for me to even hear what this three hundred-pound monstrosity of death was demanding.

Whoa! One more elbow in my face. I was prepared to fight for my life in this soundproof chamber before complying with any of his illegal requirements at this moment.

Cole, why are you messing with me? I told you that I didn't do anything bad.

Whoa! One more elbow, and then another. I felt like I was folding over, unable to maintain my balance, and heaving spit and spew out of my empty stomach from all these belly and rib shoots at one go. This continued for what seemed like hours until we were both startled by the sound of keys jingling in the holding cell door.

The cell door was wrenched open by C.O. Walker, the intake C.O., who asked if Sergeant Slaughter—another moniker for C.O. Cole—needed any assistance. It was unbelievable to me that this jerk would want to accompany him in stealing the last remnants of my innocence.

I spit out, "You dirty, fat bitch," as fast as the idea of how I was going to get back her raggedy ass for her unwanted visit occurred to me. Smirking, C.O. Cole adjusted his belt and blinked his head from left to right, giving off a loud cracking sound akin to a pack of lit Fourth of July firecrackers.

"Can I help you? I said." C.O. Walker repeated, but this time, it was unexpectedly sharper and more pointedly directed at Cold Blooded. She was there to save me, which is something that virtually seldom happens to inmates of state penitentiaries, and it was evident that day that she did not want to participate in the filthy and cruel type of time that C.O. Cole was on.

I was mistaken about C.O. Walker, just as I had been about the motives of other women who entered my life and attempted to assist me before her. I wanted so much at that time to make sure that one day she would look at me differently, not as the robber and coward I was, standing there aimlessly.

As calm as a breeze, Cold Blooded moved to the side, and it seemed as though he had changed completely. With his broad Donkey Kong shoulders, he made sure not to bump C.O. Walker as he strode past her without a word.

"All right, everybody, let's move. Return to your cell now!

I lowered my head, nodded, and put my hands behind my back. C.O. Walker took my arm as we emerged from the entryway and guided me back to my tier. Even though I knew it wasn't appropriate to say thank you, I raised my head to check whether she could sense my gratitude.

Then, a few feet ahead, observing the scene as normal, I looked up and Ray, the messenger, started acting more like a genuine person. It was logical to infer that Ray was far more powerful than I had realised, and that the big-shot C.O. Walker was his muscle on the block, capable of either saving our Black asses or killing us.

CHAPTER 8
HIGHER LEARNING

Throughout my life, I have been told countless lies, many of which have come from the men who I looked up to—the hood heroes, the men who had served time in the same prisons as me. Following years of imprisonment, these crazy men returned to their hometown and regurgitated stories more full of myth and fantasy than those found in children's novels with purple unicorns and three-headed dragons. The majority of these soldiers were always cordially welcomed back home by the town. Regardless of what they went in for, we even applauded their homecoming. However, the majority of them offered us naive young men nothing but more falsehoods and deceit.

"You're fine, young one. Until you're an adult and starting to put in some actual work, they can't give you any genuine time. If you're not blowing nobody's head off or robbing banks, you'll be straight.

That was simply one of the many falsehoods I was told to give me the impression that I could freely continue having affairs. I believed that my youth and smoothness made me unfit to endure double digit sentences among lifetime offenders. I had no idea that, little by little, I was becoming one of them. My lengthy arrest history, which began only a few days after I turned eleven, prepared me psychologically for my dramatic entrance into a life of misery.

My half-forced, half-taught ignorance quickly caught up with me, and what I had earlier considered to be child's play set me on the route to becoming a certified adult surrounded by guys who could not care less about my age or the seriousness of my actions. You were either about that life behind bars or you weren't, and if you weren't, you had better learn how to play the game like it was your last.

There were no camping trips or horseback rides to help with socialisation, trust-building, or self-esteem building like there was at Juvie. There was none of that in the prison. The programs they occasionally offered us and just being around my classmates made our time in the juvenile detention system enjoyable, even though I was unaware of it at the time. It was much easier than any day I would have spent behind bars. I had taken things for granted and, as soon as I became certified, I regretted every second of it. I think I became engrossed in the notion that I had already experienced everything and could easily go to prison if the time came. I don't think I could ever put into words how mistaken I was!

Another thing about juvie that I was unaware of being the ultimate perk was weekend passes. As long as I didn't get into any problems, I could buy myself home for the weekend and return to the school before curfew. I lost that privilege permanently the instant I stepped behind the 40-foot concrete perimeter around SCI Dallas. Nobody informs you that you are under lockdown and will be alone in a six-by-six cell for "twenty-three and one"—a period of time during which you will only hear the cries of other men who have already lost their minds and your own voice. The thoughts that weave in and out of your head like a deadly venomous snake cannot be avoided. Some of the darkest, most profound ideas have the ability to contaminate every part of your existence to the point that you end up being your own worst enemy. The hour you get to take a shower or use the phone, if you're lucky, is your only hope for comfort. Frequently, we weren't, and even in such instances, what information could we possibly have to give the person on the other end of the telephone if not lies and deceit to calm them down? similar to the elderly wise men.

I spent years rehashing the sorrow and regret of not learning my lesson before being transferred to a place where sympathy and regret were kept quieter than most secrets, from my top bunk furnished with a vinyl mattress and sheet that felt like gritty sandpaper. If you smell like a frail person, you are some crazy man's dinner in this place. I shielded myself from being seen with the tears that streamed down my face every day by using the books I claimed to read.

They ask you four questions at four separate times when you book: Have you ever received treatment for mental illness? If you take any medication at all, what is it? Do you have mental health treatment under medical supervision? How often—if at all—do you consider taking your own life? The seriousness of those questions will prick even the most rational men's mental health triggers. Before I become suicidal, how long would it take me if I wasn't already? I asked myself those kinds of questions during the soul-snatching intake procedure. And I asked myself the same question multiple times afterward, doubting my stability and occasionally feeling as though my mind was slipping away from me.

Self-inflicted insanity was the only obvious way to survive some of the most dangerous days—days when you would have preferred to be without some of your innate senses—that you could hardly have imagined. You cannot hide the thick, purple-coloured blood seeping from a man's skull, not even if you are blind. The sickening smell of a crazy prisoner hurling a milk carton full of bubbling, stewed excrement into someone's cell is unavoidable. The sound of sharpened steel slicing in and out of someone's collarbone and neck is also one you will never forget. Nothing compares to the sound of hot spikes piercing a man's jugular and his blood spurting out as he gasps for air.

It was like asking for an irreversible mental break to try to maintain composure in the face of extreme madness. It did not take long for me to realise that prison is like golf in that it is a game of opposites; however, there are no lush green acres of grass or caddies to help you carry the weight and make pivotal decisions. I constantly had to keep in mind that behind the wall, things would frequently go far left when they looked too right, and becoming very comfortable may be a deadly error. You had to always be ready to change your situation quickly because you may be someone's greatest friend one moment and their deadly adversary the next, preyed upon and looked down upon.

GETTING ON THE PHONE WAS ANOTHER RISK. You never knew what was going through someone else's life during the moments you were able to survive. Most of the people who had promised to hold you down eventually forgot about you.

Brenda stated sultrily over the phone, "I don't give a fuck what none of these motherfuckers got to say; you're my baby, Wallo." Large-Booty In the real world, Brenda was my girlfriend. She wasn't truly my girl-girl; rather, she was my piece. That one is my favourite, too. We did anything and anything you might think a couple would do to each other and for each other every time we met, even though I couldn't publicly claim her on the front streets. Brenda was an older woman (I was only thirteen when we first met) who enjoyed grooming young cats like me, cats with lots of potential to make a big splash and earn big bucks someday. She was able to spot up-and-coming talent and potential superstars, and she was adept at timing her moves to get you into the game before everyone else did.

"Yeah, but look at this, Brenda; that was all nice and stuff when we could move around as we pleased, but now I'm stuck in here with your real man, and I don't need that kind of action while I'm doing this time," I remarked in a rather harsh but subdued voice.

"Oh, so you simply call me Brenda now? When you were coming and going from my house, eating, drinking, and being fucked like the man I believed you to be, I wasn't Brenda! It was this baby, that baby. You know who the fuck put your nut ass onto all this delicious crap, but you're in a bit of a jam right now. I hope the little assholes you keep yelling at here in an attempt to get someone to sign up have something to write about because I'm pretty sure the fuck won't. You're on your own," she remarked, chuckling since she was certain she had me beat.

"Now, pause. Do you recall that you stated you had me for life? You are aware that I am unable to talk to you on the phone right now. How come you're trying to be so mean to me? You truly are my bitch; you understand how much you mean to me. Never let that stuff get misconstrued, please. I used to talk grease to her, and she liked it. She helped shape that aspect of my Philadelphia Slim persona.

Yeah, that's what I had assumed! And you better remember that because, as she half-jokingly warned, "We're going to have a problem if I hear about one more of these little hoes talking about you putting them on your visitation list."

Yes, B, please shut up and make sure you post something on my account today. If you don't, I'll screw about and miss the store till the following week. You better make sure your favorite nigga gets to eat because you know my skinny-ass ribs are already touching.

Without sharing a single encouraging remark, not even a "I love you," or anything indicative of a strong, loving relationship, we hung up. We didn't come from it, so none of that was ever taken into consideration. These were the fleeting moments of love experienced only by those raised in wholesome, honourable, and intact households. None of those things described us. I was her plaything, a follower of her teachings, and a do-boy who obeyed her orders because her hand demanded it. She was a gangster, a pimp, and a lady of the night.

Speaking with Brenda seemed like going back in time to my childhood, when I was naive, carefree, and possessing the kind of obstinate ignorance that seemed to elude time, conventions, laws, and limits. I wasn't always sure if I was controlling the game more—her or me. Even when she was blatantly incorrect, that bitch always understood what was appropriate to say. She was cunning and quick-witted, and not much got past her. She had a way with words. But when I first saw her, it was her body that drew my attention. She resembled an athlete in the track and field events who overindulged in red velvet slices. She was juicy and jiggling thick, with just the proper amount of muscular tone. Her legs resembled cushions, silky as satin. She completely turned me on like she was the daughter of Satan, I can't even lie!

I could still vividly recall Brenda driving her ivory-white Mercedes-Benz with matching driving gloves and chinchilla fur trim through the neighbourhood during the winter. She was the ideal woman for a drug dealer. If there was one thing about her that was constantly in demand, it was money—everything about her, from head to toe, was exclusive. Few women from our side of Philadelphia had as much success as she did. Of course, there were the fly gals that lived in the background who could pull off some fly things from the hot boys, like an occasional Coach or Gucci purse or pair of shoes. That expensive stuff, however, wasn't as simple to obtain as it was for Brenda.

Those females were in fact in need of labour. They couldn't just relax, gather their treasures, and look adorable. No, before they could even consider looking through a fashion book, they had to get their asses up, bust moves like mules, and make some things happen for their dealer daddies up and down 95 South. No matter how fly they were, those were the gals who were either getting robbed by their sidepiece partners, the ones who had time to show them a little attention, or they were getting knocked down by the feds for talking too much and acting too ostentatious. Not Brenda, that is. She was unique and unlike any of them!

In the dim light of flickering fluorescent corner store lights and gloomy street lamps, Brenda parked her car twice and signalled with her hazards on, as though she was expecting someone or something to approach. It was a chilly November night. The spotless rays that gleamed from her rims like light from a chandelier let me know it was her. Those shits were always spotless, as if we didn't live in a city with four distinct seasons, with snow and black ice remnants from the previous few nights still visible. The way Shorty handled her handle was simply flawless. As I ate a bag of Doritos and drank an orange drink, I tried not to look suspicious while noticing how wealthy and out of place she always seemed to be. I couldn't stop staring as I imagined myself thumping my cousin Gillie's music through the system while driving that automobile with the seat back. I could only see them perspiring uncontrollably as I pulled up in a Big Body Benz. The sound of a high-pitched beep emanating from Brenda's pager via her window abruptly cut through that vision. She could afford to have the heat turned up high enough to let in some crisp air without worrying about wasting gas, because I saw she kept the windows cracked. Oh my goodness, I thought to myself, this bitch is awful.

Her pager went off again after a little interval. She was searching the area between the passenger seat and the dashboard, as I could see. We met eye to eye, and I almost choked as she looked up and out the window. She made sure I knew she had seen me looking, even though I attempted to quickly turn away so she wouldn't think I was up to something.

She remarked, "Aye, little man, come here; let me give you something to do," as she depressed her window with a button. I pointed to myself while looking around in confusion. She cried, "Yeah, come get this bread."

"Young man?" I fired back. I've always had a problem with labels that didn't match my true self-perception or ability.

Saying, "Boy, please, forget it, I'll do it myself," she gritted her teeth. I ran and was leaning at the passenger-side window waiting for her to tell me what she needed as soon as she started to get out of her car.

"Hello, may I ask your name? Given that it's evident you dislike the moniker "Little Man," she remarked with a small smile.

Wallo, I muttered, straining to make my voice sound deeper.

"Wallo? That name, what kind is it?

I made that up off the top of my head and said, "It's short for Wallace Rocks a Lot of Polo."

She reached out and said, "Oh okay, Wallo, open your hand." "Try to get the corner store to give you some change using this beeper and a few dollars. Use the change to give them a call back from the pay phone when the beeper from the 704 area code goes off, and let them know you'll be waiting for them to drop off the work.

"Huh?" As I tried to take in what she had just said, I asked.

Wallo, come on, you heard what I said—this crap is fundamental! I did, but I felt dazed and disoriented.

"Why don't you just use that big-block cell phone that you just took out from under the passenger seat?" I inquired.

"You got a lot to learn, Little Man," she hissed, shaking her head and sucking her teeth once more before grabbing the gear change and pulling off, seemingly ready to leave me for dead.

I leaned back, my expression snarly. Hey, this is Wallo. Why the fuck are you expecting me to perform this task when I'm so small? Shit, Ms. Whatever-Your-Name-Is, I don't even know you that way.

"You're right, Wallo, my bad," she added, chuckling a little. On the other hand, I've heard some major league trash about your dad from folks I know. You have some pretty large shoes to fill, so I'm simply watching out for you and lending a hand a little.

It didn't take me long at all to jump on board. One thing about Philadelphia is that word spreads quickly. This is a place where not too much crap stays low. It made no difference if it was good, horrible, or neutral. A word about where you got it or how loud it was would get out if you were making a little noise or had a dollar in your pocket anywhere from here to downtown.

My father's name stuck in the air long enough for the generations that followed him to be familiar with at least a few anecdotes. I would be a two-bit fool, jumping through hoops at the mere mention of his name. The legend of my pop dukes was the only person I looked up to.

When Brenda brought up my pedigree, she was undoubtedly speaking from experience. And if she wasn't aware at the time, she was aware very soon as I became her most devoted soldier very rapidly. I had a big chip on my shoulder and had a thing to prove.

Following a breakup with Brenda I paused, taking a long breath out, and then I walked back to my cell. I could feel my head looming over my slouched shoulders. After spewing my stuff over the phone, I wasn't my normal hyperactive self, so anyone with half an eye could see I was in a mood.

A gang member named Big June screamed, "Look at this limp noodle, got caught up fantasy-mac n on the jack; now he can't hold his neck up," from across the room. My gaze swerved over the space, piercing him like a laser. My pulse was pounding like a cokehead and my blood was already boiling. Though I hadn't always been so easily enraged, I started to feel more and more like a victim as time went on and I was living in the filthy dungeon that was now my home.

I shot out at him, "Yo, June, mind your fucking business." Suddenly, I noticed a flash of light within him. He seems to have been waiting for any opportunity to turn the tables on me. If the chance arose, it would only take anything so small, so unimportant, some shit he started to make me want to fight with him.

Luckily, when shit was ready to pop off, there were two guards circling the area. Until there was anything serious going on and you wanted to get out by being put in the hole, no one was foolish enough to set it off with the law in place. Although neither of us took it seriously, it was clear that Big June wanted a fight with me and that it would soon get out of hand. Just not at that particular moment.

I was lonely and wanted to be alone in my cell. Some days, I would rather spend time alone with my thoughts in the dayroom or outside in the yard. Money could not buy peace and quiet, so when my bunky happened to be free one day, I would use the opportunity to go through my mental crates. Who am I to fool? This wasn't the usual occasion when I would have party time with a handcrafted fifi bag that was moistened and a smut mag when I had the cell to myself. Perhaps Big June was correct. It's not supposed to happen, but I was fantasy-mac n on the line, and it took me right into my emotions.

Selling dreams is the goal of fantasy-mac'n, not acquiring them. Sometimes the macintosh becomes so excellent that you begin to believe your own garbage. While every man incarcerated has a tale to tell, the true fantasy-macs are the ones who can sell water to a whale. As far as I understood, some big-time macs had as many as twenty women at a time under the impression that they would be coming home in a few months at most, and that they would lay them out with houses and diamonds and furs, provided they stayed tight and restrained. Believe it or not, the pleasant sound of an appeal kept a gang of fantasy-macs' commissaries stocked, even though the majority of them faced a twenty-to-life sentence.

"Hey, man, you heard that bullshit shouldn't trip you up?"

Hearing Mitch say that while jokingly standing in front of our cell startled me. Seated on my bunk, I gave him the impression that I had no idea what he was talking about.

What do you mean? "Travelling on what?"

"They told me you've been hiding in your bunk like a little hoe and that you and Big June were about to bump heads a few minutes ago," he chuckled. I also chuckled.

I said, "Nope, just chilling and thinking about some stuff, that's all, man."

Mitch said, "Oh, okay, you know if shit gets too crazy I got you," and he turned to leave.

"Yeah, I'm cool though, real shit," I said, trying to sound unperturbed.

Honestly, I wasn't at all bothered by Big June at that particular moment because I had gotten lost in my memories and nearly forgot where I was lying. My thoughts had been free to wander for little more than twenty minutes, during which time I felt a sense of illusory freedom.

I had to summon all my strength to prevent pure terror from taking over. I leaped from my bunk and doused my face with water from the corroded steel basin. At this point, I made the decision to grab a pen and begin penning my "Letters to Freedom." I was aware that there would be no other way for me to win this bid without going crazy.

CHAPTER 9
STAYIN' ALIVE

If I claimed that I wasn't actively engaged in the illegal enterprise while inside, I would be lying to you. Whether you like it or not, no one gets off so easily that you don't have to earn your place. When incarcerated, there is always a trade-off for your life. Depending on the energy you put out there, some people will have it far worse than others—like what happened to Red. He ended up dead in a six-by-six prison cell, his ass blown out, and he went around looking tough with his chest protruding. Please understand that I'm not blaming Red for what transpired; rather, I'm stating that different energies elicit particular reactions, and in that setting, taking on particular roles was akin to tossing a die. I've never played the tough guy. That would get me exactly what I knew it would. If you take on that position, you will be tested and examined frequently until you either find a body or someone takes it away from you.

My involvement in the criminal circles had remained hidden up to this point. There had not been a single instance where I was apprehended or exposed for my involvement in any actions that would have resulted in a longer term. I would like to think that I avoided detection because I was sly, but I'm convinced that God had other intentions. Instead, I played a cruel game of cat and mouse with the authorities. You've heard the saying, "God shields fools and infants." Finding methods to help the group of cells holding me down wasn't always simple, but I made the decision to serve in a way that required less danger and paid off more, that much is certain.

Pretending to be the go-between for a commissary bully and a rookie prisoner who had the necessary support structure to get through his days unscathed was one of the most satisfying tricks I would play.

When an inmate was being processed for the first time, or if they were being transferred from another prison and were getting punched before they reached our cellblock, I would say, "Aye, man, I don't know what you did to get green-lit, but once you got that target on your back, you're about to have a real fucked-up time in here unless you comply." The objective of the game was to keep the bullies off the rookie's ass while making some money for our cells by negotiating commissary money and contraband smuggled in by one of his family members or friends. Surprisingly enough, even though it was still flawed, I thought this plan was honourable because it prevented the inexperienced players from being thrown in. Having someone stand between him and a crazy man who was shaking him down was consoling for the newjack. However, on the other hand, I was participating in the extortion of someone's family, who would do anything to protect their loved one, even if it meant jeopardising their own freedom by sneaking illegal goods into the country while they were visiting.

The good thing was that I didn't face many dangers when making these purchases. I gave the impression of being the mediator—a kind of hero. The drawback was the moral burden it carried, knowing that someone's expectant wife had transported drugs in their baby girl's diaper to pay for my protection and to keep him safe from those who would have killed him.

It was always a game of opposites, much like golf. When I looked at it, it seemed like I was accomplishing three goals at once, and nobody was harmed unless they were discovered. For me at the time, this exemplified what it meant to be "armed with good intentions." I had the advantage of being affable in circumstances where others might have felt compelled to use coercion thanks to the con game.

Listen up: Anyone who ever believed that incarceration was a place where people may reform is sorely incorrect. When your daily livelihood depends on bargaining, what other talent would you have to rely on if your entire foundation has been constructed on illegal intentions? That's one of the main causes of the frequent turnover. You enter and unintentionally discover how to become a more cunning crook.

I've read a lot and looked up suggestions for things to do after I get out during the last two months. I developed an obsession with marketing since it was like playing a scam, only it wasn't illegal. I began using some of the techniques I had read about in master marketing books on some prison officials, between extortion tactics and acting as a middleman. I reasoned that I could definitely market myself to the parole board in a way that would make them believe the crap I was selling if I could learn how to sell fresh concepts and alter their viewpoint.

Now let's get real: The board is not interested in hearing people's heartbreaking tales of how their father abandoned them and made them feel unworthy of a man when they grew up. No. Whether or if you were genuinely guilty of the crime you were imprisoned for, they want you to wear it on your chest. They want you to repent with every breath because they are bloodthirsty. They want you to demonstrate that you have changed and that your decision to serve time was the worst thing you have ever done. They want you to plead for your freedom without seeming like you're pleading, because, God forbid, you would genuinely be willing to grovel for it. If so, you would be considered unfit and might possibly be prescribed mental health medication.

I realised that in order to at least find out what it takes to placate those assholes on the parole board, I had to plan ahead and grease every word I uttered at my parole meeting. I thus read till my eyes were bloodshot while staying up late. I knew better than to get my hopes up on my first home walk before the board, so I was mentally prepared to be refused parole. However, I was also ready to shake the tree of information and determine precisely which phrases and nonverbal cues favoured me. At this point, the game was losing, but the numerous hours of preparation were worthwhile in order to acquire the knowledge.

IN BETWEEN THE TIMES I DID my new-found fascination with reading and study, and occasionally I would just daydream while drifting off to sleep in my bunk, and Brenda would almost seem like a ghost of times past. We'd call it getting lost in the sauce. dreaming while keeping your eyes open. Not quite awake, but not quite asleep either.

Although Brenda wasn't the only girl I fell hard for, the truth is that, to be honest, she was the worst of all of them. To be honest, I'm not sure if she was really my girl. When I think of how gone I was off that lady, I have to giggle. Brenda had a grown man serving time in the pen before I was put up, and I used to be silent whenever she had to answer a collect call from him. She was holding down her genuine nigga until his time was up, and I guess I was just his sidekick. I was enjoying every benefit and reward he was missing, so I couldn't give less of a fuck. We would resume work as soon as she hung up with the idiot, as if he had never even happened.

Brenda purred like a kitten and said, "Lo baby, hand me that jar of honey; let me show you something." After a while, you got to know her and realised it was just her typical tone. Whether it was sweet transactions, pickups and drops, or some freaky sexual shit she would be kicking on the phone with her boo in the clink, she was always so polished in her delivery of everything. Her voice sounded like the sensuous, silky murmur of a snake charmer from the ghetto.

We used to just kick it for hours at her condo downtown. She would introduce me to all the newest high-end items that season, whether they were furnishings, clothing, shoes, or anything else that caught her interest. Brenda used to lick the tip of her finger, slide it down the ear of every magazine page she really liked, then fold it at the corner to help her remember where her next expensive purchases would come from. That stuff was smooth and would get me excited.

"Baby, keep up the wonderful work. One day, she would say, "You'll have a place just like this too."

"I prefer it just the way it is; I don't need any of this flashy shit. If you continue to allow me to work, I'll write my paper and get my mother and Nanny a new home. To cover up my embarrassing behaviour, I would remark, "I guarantee you, I'm supercool on all that. Naturally, I wanted more for myself, but I also realised that the path I was on wouldn't last. I detested never being able to assume the full role of a professional drug dealer. One of the main reasons I felt little about it was the knowledge that I would never be able to follow in my father's footsteps in the drug trade.

I brought the jar of honey she had requested when I came back from the kitchen. She moved all of her seasonings and condiments into prettier containers so you wouldn't see the awful store labels, and I was really impressed by that. I used the little things that I learned from her simple presence in various aspects of my life. I discovered that some coloured and packaged baggies were visually appealing and appeared to attract the dope gang members back to my mother's porch for a quick re-up more quickly than others.

Brenda never seemed to take much of a shot at me. She was aware that I wasn't suited to be a kingpin and didn't want me to be one. I was gleefully glad to be around, pick up some games, and stack some cash, much like a small dog. She had different plans for me.

Brenda was wearing only her underwear and an emerald-green lace bra when I returned to her room. My favourite colour is green. To be honest, I didn't know if she gave a damn or even knew. I had been waiting patiently until this very moment. We hadn't really done anything save a few occasional tugs and rubs up until now. I never thought she would genuinely be interested in me enough to follow through.

"Please come here and take a nap." She caressed her pink satin queen-size sheets. I thought I was in over my head as I stepped over and sat on the edge of the bed.

"Nuh-uh, remove those trendy street clothes! We don't act like that here," she screamed.

I undressed quicker than Clark Kent could metamorphose into Superman. She grabbed me by the shoulders and made me lie down. Oh sh*t, I thought. This is going to get serious. No matter how big of a horndog you are in these situations, let me tell you—there's a strange vulnerability that comes with being told what to do while lying in a submissive posture with a lady who has 10 times more life experience than you.

I can still clearly recall lying back and tightly closing my eyes. Then, I awoke to find myself completely covered in honey. Brenda was giving me kisses and sucking honey off every part of my body. My eyes sprung open at the warmth of her mouth and the stickiness of her honey-coated lips when she reached my whip. I needed to see for myself what kind of sorcery she was doing to me. I'm in shock over this! I could really get into this bitch!

I had to come back to reality as I heard the noise of prisoners entering from the yard. Once more, I closed my eyes and tried to hold onto the image of Brenda and myself for as long as I could. Perhaps it was too long because, in that moment, I caught a vision in my mind of my thirteen-year-old, sensually aroused naked body.

My inner voice said, "I was just a kid," as I experienced sickness that tore at my stomach. Prisoners began to shambolically and loudly make their way along the tier, diverting my attention from a discovery that I sorely needed to digest. At the time, Brenda was just under thirty years old.

Was she a child molester? I shook my head and murmured. "How come it feels so wrong now, when it felt so right before?" Well, that didn't feel right at the time, either. I was just content with my sense of manhood and my ability to get away with things. However, I wasn't. Indeed, she was. "My naiveté," I exclaimed.

"Young Bul, what's the word?" A well-known voice interrupted my perplexed thoughts. Ray's voice could be heard coming from my cell's entrance. Though his tone was upbeat, his countenance suddenly shifted. I sat up and he saw the serious expression on my face, and his normally placid expression changed to one of anxiety. "Yes, sir, are you okay? He replied, "You look like you just saw a ghost," as he peered over his shoulder to see if any prisoners were approaching. One prisoner can only express so much compassion for another before unfounded rumours of funny business begin to circulate.

"Shit, damn near," I shot back, forcing myself to swallow hard to keep from throwing my ramen all over the jail.

Ray said, "Shake that shit off," without even trying to find out what was wrong. "Go outside and leave what's outside! Have you heard of it? One day at a time, you can only address what is directly in front of you. He hesitated, shaking an envelope in his palm, then said, "Besides, the messenger man just brought you some good news."

I leaped to my feet and almost grabbed the package from his grasp.

I stood there in disbelief that I had passed my GED exam, and he remarked, "Good job, my boy!"

"Oh my god. "Man, we did this shit!" I said.

You did that, though. Ray remarked, "You put your head down, read those books like I instructed, and you came to your own conclusion.

I was overcome with perplexity and a tug of conflicting feelings. I was initially taken aback by this news. On the other hand, I had never even contemplated the fact that I had been sexually abused as a child until I just came to that realisation. I tried to stay present and shook my head. However, I could tell Ray was aware of my conflicting feelings based on the expression on his face.

"Well, congratulations, young one," he remarked, reaching out a hand to shake hands, and then making his way back to his cell.

It's not really appropriate to seek clarity on matters in prison, especially those related to sexuality, so I wasn't going to let Ray into my private thoughts in that way. The majority of males recount these tales with their chests bared as a sign of respect. Once, when I didn't think there was anything wrong with the nasty things that were going on, I did the same thing.

I would fuck and sling packs for a kingpin's old woman, telling all the men back in the juvenile prison building how I was popping my ass. I told those stories with pride, as if I was actually out there doing something worthy of stripes, even though I'm confident that more than half of them thought I was bullshit.

61

The very thought of it made my palms clammy. I clutched the fruits of my labour and devotion in one hand. I was grinning, thinking, Wow, I passed my GED. Using my other hand, I pressed on my face, attempting to erase the collection of soiled recollections of being duped by a lady.

I made the decision to not let the ominous clouds cast a shadow over me and dim the enthusiasm I had from my excellent response. I shrugged it off, thinking this would be a perfect opportunity to call home and tell Jackie the wonderful news.

I had many questions about aspects of my life that I felt I had to come to terms with as I left my cell, envelope still in hand. Every few steps, I would stop and wonder where my mother was at any given time. I wondered if I even had the right to question her when I was the one making all the bad choices. There was a distinct emotion with each step. With the right step, I felt abandoned and victimised, and with the left, I was clearly stone-cold trippin'. You are a drug dealer, dog, and you got some ass off your mother's porch. What the devil is wrong with it, anyway? By the time I got to the phone, I had so many questions for myself that I realised calling my mother wasn't the right thing to do.

CHAPTER 10
HIT DOGS HOLLER

One day, a few big heads burst into the building, tearing through each cell on each floor, looking like crazed hounds for smut mags and contraband. Stormtroopers turned our beds over, toppled the shelves containing our family photos, and pillaged all we had left personally, as if nothing mattered. Hundreds of prisoners screamed, "Fuck the cops," and other insane things they could think of, but it was pretty much their only option. There rarely too much opposition to the huge hats. Their power is quicker than that of the regular C.O.s, so if you're not careful, you could find yourself in the hole for at least a year merely seeming crazy. It's best not to tamper with the large caps. All the time!

We referred to the warden and his group of senior officials as big hats. Not the small ones with the ridiculous, knockoff cardboard-like hats we had to deal with on a daily basis, but the ultimate dickheads. These motherfuckers would occasionally find a new issue to pick fights with us about. This time, for some reason, smut mags and anything featuring a chubby man and some titties were the target audience. Wanting to punish a man more while he's already receiving punishment is twisted and sick. Today saw the passing of a new regulation that said that any sexual content discovered on the property would be deemed contraband and would result in a strike against you. A hit is merely another way to punish someone for further punishing someone else, like a jail inside a prison, or a hole created just for minding your own business.

One level after another, the cell blocks were rocked by the unexpected news of the new regulation. Their plan was to get rid of the last trace of these two thousand guys who had been kept in those cages for years, some even for life, without seeing, feeling, or smelling like women. This scum needed to be punished cruelly and unusually. Shouts from sweltering prisoners reverberated through the levels, sending waves of nervous looks and rumours of late-night uprisings once the large hats were taken off.

But Mitch and I were lucky; our cell had been cleansed of everything else before they arrived, save for a few of black-tail magazines featuring Pinky, my all-time favourite freak hoe. Goddamn, it was such a special house. Thankfully, though, our cell did not include any drugs, shanks, or anything unusual that would have made my life unbearable.

Red was dead, and we were all placed under strict lockdown. For weeks, we had to adhere to a rigid twenty-three-and-one. There was no yard, no visitors, and sometimes it would take days to be allowed outside to take a shower. It was inevitable that there would be fights, stabbings, and rapes while incarcerated. However, they had to stop everything, including medical care, as soon as the warden learned that Red's bodily cavity was filled with more than a hundred different medications. After concluding that the amount of narcotics coming in could not possibly be coming from the streets, they were forced to launch internal investigations against every employee, starting with the officers and ending with the nurses, in order to prevent the media from learning about it.

There was no better time for the cell raids to occur. Lockdown prevented me from having to take over and start carrying all the drugs and crap Red was too old to do. I was able to start considering how to make my stay here more comfortable if I wasn't going to be leaving anytime soon because I didn't have to worry about getting sucked into some significant work that I didn't want to be involved in.

I had participated in every program the state provided for the previous eighteen months in an effort to set myself up for an early release. When I was able to apply for the programs, which was twenty-three months before my minimum term, I made it my mission to get on the list as quickly as possible. My old friends didn't seem as enthusiastic or confident in the program as I did at the time, so I asked around and talked to them about the application process and what I could do to improve my chances. The majority of them chuckled and referred to me as a novice, and without hesitation, they reminded me that I was a repeat offender and that the odds were not in my favour.

I was unable to adopt their way of thinking. I reasoned that because we had nothing to lose, why not give it a shot? I was certain that time would pass anyhow, so I might as well take advantage of the opportunity and, if nothing else, pick up some new knowledge.

That night, falling asleep wasn't going to be simple. I had barely twenty-four hours to find out if I was allowed to blow this joint or not—the state makes its choice several months after my parole hearing. My neck hurt from all the tossing and turning I was doing. I was restless. Tired in my mind, I lay on my back and traced the ceiling cracks, visualising each twisting one as a path leading back to Nanny's house.

I wasn't really helped by jogging down memory lane because it made me question why I was in such a rush to return outside. Naturally, as soon as I set foot on the ground, I was surrounded by luxury—money, cars, hoes, and freedom—but I hadn't really thought through a strategy that would keep me out of trouble in the future. I was certain that I would release a mixtape. I had less than twenty-four hours before I saw the early release counsellor, and I'm very sure that rapping wouldn't be a compelling enough job description for her to sign the approval form. I had too much to say, to put it mildly. I just had one idea for the eighteen months I had left to sort it out: I was going to release a mixtape, create clothing, and do a ton of other things that black people in my neighbourhood had never done. Was this just one more set up to go wrong? I had to ask myself.

It was common knowledge, even for me, that aiming for an early release on your first try would only lead to disaster. Nevertheless, I let the thought of returning home stab me in the heart with deadly accuracy. Even if it appeared that I had adapted nicely to life in prison, that was all a front. I wanted to get out of there because I had developed ulcers in my stomach from struggling with the idea of having to pay for my mistakes with my life.

Please release me. Please release me. Please release me.

I closed my eyes tightly, attempting to drown out the cries for help I was hearing in my head, asking God or anyone else who would listen to save me from this terrible place. Before I understood what they were, panic attacks had a funny way of surprising me with unexpected attacks. The panic was so strong that I could feel myself giving up the struggle to its repetitive rhythm of constant pleading. I felt my hands close to crushing my skull as I clutched my head with both of them. I was thinking so loudly about my panic that I was unable to focus. It was as though my own frenzy was coming from a loudspeaker. I was pretty convinced I could hear everyone. My palms started to perspire, my throat felt like it was closing, and my breathing get shallow. I was getting more anxious by the second as time was running out. I can't recall ever having to silence the voice in my head or having it be this loud.

And then, BOOM BOOM, just when I thought I could be suffering a heart attack. I was terrified to death by two loud noises that came from under my bunk. After again kicking me out of my bunk, Mitch angrily exclaimed, "Cut that shit out, man." You are already aware of what is going to occur.

I sat there, trying to process what he had said, perspiring. He was correct, and I felt a surge of rage as well, realising that I had just let myself get carried away with a silly illusion.

Hey, you're really getting off my nerves, I thought to myself. I was conscious that I was tripping at that very moment, and it caused me to lose my hold on reality and myself. My head was blown up by hope's audacity, and the only thing keeping it from going too far into my skull was to chuckle at how foolish I was to let hope choke me.

When it came time for the morning count, I had hardly slept for two or three hours, yet I felt incredibly energised, almost like I was excited about something. That morning, I couldn't help but notice the expression on Mitch's face. It seemed as though he found my nervousness repulsive, or worse. I pondered whether he had begun to subtly despise me. What if he resented that it was me and not him, and he believed I had a shot of an early release? I grasped my head firmly with both hands once more, dismissing the bothersome ideas and realised that this new, invading voice in my head was beginning to become a challenge that I needed to face. I'm actually having a great time, man. Come together!

I couldn't help but reflect on the effort and time it had taken for me to get here. Based on the information found in my files, I should have been regarded as successful in the programs I had participated in. I kept my record spotless and did a respectable job in the kitchen, even if it was just chopping up countless amounts of potatoes. I thought I was due to return home.

According to what I've heard, parole or early release programs are basically numbers games, and nobody really cares if you served your time with honour or not. Under an early release program, you are released from prison to a halfway house rather than serving out the remainder of your term. Fifty heads would be released at random if they had to make room for fifty more inmates in order to release fifty beds. I've heard of kitties who made huge mistakes getting accepted, and individuals with spotless backgrounds who had completed multiple programs being turned down. It was just a case of bad luck. But whether you're a perfect gentleman or not, nine times out of ten, your initial attempt is effectively rejected.

I was certain that I would not be consuming any food from the chow hall. I could just as easily screw about and piss myself on the way to the council meeting. I started to feel as though my stomach was about to fall out from under me because my nerves were so high. I've witnessed other bulls experience that as well; their stomachs became so messed up before they met the board that they crap the ground.

In addition, I didn't want anything or anybody to make me lose focus. Since I was on high alert, I made the decision to stop eating and doing everything else until it was time for me to visit and find out the outcome. I spent a lot of time thinking about my brother Steven and how our current lives might end before we have a chance to make a difference while I waited.

I sat waiting for the time to pass on the paint-chipped, frigid stool that was attached to the thin metal desk of the cell. I considered drafting a letter to Freedom, but I was too preoccupied with worrying about my future. I surveyed my cell in the hopes that anything would grab my attention and divert me from this memory lane once more. Not right now.

When I told the intake counsellors at the juvenile detention camps that I liked to snort up a fifty-piece of coke once a week for fun, I recalled lying through my teeth. That was the deepest deception imaginable. No matter how much fun some of Steven's older pals made it sound, I didn't have the balls to do it. I was occasionally inclined to prove that I was just as cool as them. However, I was always too perceptive and witnessed directly what it did to my people. I saw how swiftly it changed the people around me that I looked up to, and how it changed them virtually overnight.

What made me tell those juvie counsellors a lie, then? Because there were benefits associated with being labelled as a drug user or addict inside the facilities, such as extra time spent talking sh*t with counsellors about utterly pointless things and access to unique activities and programs. Anything was preferable to being completely bored while sitting in your dorm. I reasoned that I would just make up a story to take advantage of the little phoney pity they still had, which was usually reserved for crack babies and junior dust heads.

Every action and word I spoke came from a need to survive. "Play a sucker to catch a sucker," which is Law 21 from 48 Laws of Power, is what I lived by. I never cared if I played less intelligent than my mark. I was, therefore, a cokehead as long as there was a prize.

The sound of an officer yelling my name over the PA system signalled the end of my time travel. I didn't anticipate being called to the counsellor's office until later in the afternoon because it was still early. Suddenly, I felt nauseated once more, like though the ramen from last night would make me throw up. I would have assumed that my ankles were chained to the desk if I hadn't known any different. It felt like I was walking through quicksand the way I was moving.

"Well, screw it," I murmured. "Let's just finish this so I can return to working on my time without having to listen to these begging-ass voices in my head." However, there was another part of me that wondered how I would react to the news in the event that I was given my release. I could imagine myself yelling like a scratch-off lottery winner or prostitute. I laughed so hard at the prospect of that that I got a few looks from individuals who thought I was crazy.

Please take a seat.

Entering, I mean-mugged my way to the wooden desk and waited, almost as if I wanted my denial slip. That's how much I wanted to shield myself from the negative fallout if it turned out that I made the wrong choice.

"Inmate Peeples, the State of Pennsylvania has determined that you are eligible for an early release. After this meeting, your awaiting release will be scheduled in thirty days. You will have to live in a halfway home for the next year, and you will have to work for pay until the end of the time you have been given, no matter how many days it takes. Mr. Peeples, are you understanding me?

I froze. I was unable to speak, hear, move, or think.

"People, is that understood?"

Yes, indeed, I did understand! Yes, ma'am, I mean it.

It was unbelievable to me that, on my very first try, I had been given early parole and was one of those lucky random motherfuckers. I felt like screaming, pleading, and going to my knees. I had to be reminded that certain things are better left unsaid and that good news doesn't always travel well behind these walls because I was overcome with emotion.

We discussed the conditions that needed to be met in order for me to be released from custody as well as the obligations I had to the state. By then, I was so engrossed in the moment that I couldn't have cared less what the counsellor had to say. She may as well have been speaking a different language. I could practically feel the cool, fresh breeze and the sun on my face in my imagination. I knew that my cousin Gillie would be the first person I needed to call. He would see to it that, on the day of my release, I had a clean outfit ready.

I did not read a word of the documentation I signed. With a faint laugh, the counsellor wished me luck.

"Ms. Umm, Ms. Umm, Counselor, thank you!"

"Mr. Peeples, I hope I never see you again!"

I was so delighted that I was at a loss for words, yet the happiness left me as soon as it appeared. Upon leaving the workplace, I had the impression that everyone was staring at me, and not in a good way. The feeling that I would be returning to my cell through a minefield was something I was unprepared for.

It felt like there was a line of ravenous wolves waiting for any excuse to let go, and I was the food—even though I was confident no one had overheard the news that had been delivered to me.

I was to remain out of the way for at least thirty days.

A long time ago, the wise men told me that cats would attempt to deceive me into giving up my independence. To give the state an excuse to back out of their agreement to free me and keep my ass imprisoned here, they would start some stuff with me. I kept my head down and put on a mean poker look as I made my way down the hallways because there was no way I was going to allow it to happen. I even avoided using the phones to give the impression that I had no need to call home.

Everyone was moving on to their next location as Chow was nearing an end. The fact that a small group of prisoners were being led through the central area in a chain-gang fashion indicated that this was probably a transfer from one prison to another.

I paused instantly after getting past them due to a delayed reaction. I thought to myself, "I know that can't be him," but when I turned around, my initial impression was validated: There stood Baby D, shackled from ankle to ankle, gazing back at me.

I said, "Oh sh*t, how are you?" I'm hoping my look of amazement escaped his notice.

Although we both nodded to indicate what was going on, the C.O. could sense the tension between us.

The cop yelled at Baby D, "Turn the fuck around, newbie." I started running without warning, the same way I had the last time I saw him, as he turned his head back toward the direction they were travelling.

It was quiet on the streets; it had been years since anyone had heard from Baby D. There were rumours that he was either out of the picture in another state, dead, or hog-tied in someone's cellar. I was never too curious to find out or ask questions. Wherever he was, it still didn't seem far enough away to me. But here he was at last. Perhaps he was brought to our state via extradition from wherever he fled. In any case, I didn't want anything to do with him, and even though I still don't fully understand what actually transpired that evening, I don't want to find out.

I had thirty days to avoid anything or anyone that could take me off my square. That was all I had.

I have thirty days to come up with a plan to tour with Cousin Gill and blow up my mixtape.

I was shocked to learn that I only had thirty days to clear my head and leave this place.

It felt like a year was coming during those thirty days.

CHAPTER 11
FRESH AIR

When I was prepared to be honest about my release date, rumours that I was leaving had already begun to circulate. I attempted to persuade other individuals that I wasn't sure whether I had been approved and that one of the higher-ups was holding up my papers, but the majority of them had heard similar lies from others and knew I was faking. The bright side is that I didn't meet any deadly opponents while I was there. I can honestly say that God had to have been on my side for me to have dodged so many awkward circumstances that others would not have survived. I clowned and tap danced my way out of plenty of embarrassing situations that could have cost me my life.

I was about to be released from prison after two weeks when I got a note saying Baby D wanted to talk to me.

I wouldn't be telling the truth if I said I wasn't sure how to take the note. I didn't get the impression from Baby D's remarks that everything was perfect, especially considering how things stopped years ago, because they weren't explicit enough. A hint of paranoia crept in, and I felt queasy at the possibility that what he had said was a covert threat. I would have been gone long before they brought Baby D back to the general public, therefore I couldn't have been a happier nigga at that point.

Back in the library, I had become acquainted with a man named Rick over the course of the previous few months as I busied myself reading books on motivation, self-help, and anything else I could get my hands on to keep myself busy and out of trouble. Rick was an elderly feline, estimated to be in his late fifties; his skin tone was maple-brown, and his beard was neatly cut and tapered. I couldn't bring myself to tell him that he made me think of my dad. It was difficult for me to try to understand that sensation for myself. I imagined my father would be like this if he were still living at his age. Rick was quiet and polished, and it seemed like he was always trying to figure out something. He reminded me of my father in a way—a cold, collected genius.

Before I checked it out, I once unintentionally picked up one of the books he had put on the table next to my pile. The Spook Who Sat by the Door was the title of the book. "My bad," I said as I set it back down after realising it wasn't mine.

"Nah, that one is for you," Rick shot back. Try it out and let us know what you think.

I turned the pages of the book from front to back, feigning interest in the blurb, but in reality, I had no desire to read a work of fiction. Rick said, "Give it a try and see what you think," clearly seeing through my charade.

I chuckled. "Okay, okay, cool, I'll give it a try."

Rick gave a nod and resumed perusing the shelves.

I never was good at fiction. It took me a while to enjoy reading on my own, and I thought fiction was a waste of time.

I soon discovered the real significance of the adage "never judge a book by its cover" after reading the first few chapters. I gave it my all. I had a hard time believing this book was fiction because it included so many relatable elements about our neighbourhoods. I read it in four days, which is a record for me, and I was eager to share my feelings with Rick.

When we reconnected in the library a few days later, I couldn't wait to tell Rick how influential I felt the book had been. I took a seat across the table from him and began babbling about how the book transported me to a neighbourhood I had never been to before. After hearing me out for a bit, Rick inquired, "What did you learn about yourself?" while maintaining eye contact with me.

"What about me?" I questioned. "No, I didn't. What exactly was I meant to discover about myself, after all?

"Firstly, how to be a leader."

"Yeah, I understand that part."

Rick shook his head, looking at me. You know, I really do see a lot of myself in you. You're a kind child, yet you lack initiative. I'm not here to lecture you, but in my twenty years in prison, I've discovered that followers are fools. People seem to chat when they see you around. Your impulses are weak, but your heart is wonderful. And if you're not careful, you'll find yourself back here, and each time you return, the encounter will be unique. There are those that are worse than others.

I agreed with a nod and reflected on how fortunate I had been to avoid some of the experiences I had seen other prisoners go through.

"Why are you in this place?" I enquired.

Rick fell asleep as though he had returned to the day his life was irrevocably altered by his error. "I went on a run, I had no business going on," he said after taking a deep breath. I was just hanging out with two of my pals when they made the decision to rob a liquor store. The store clerk pulled out a revolver as Shit went left. An elderly man, his nerves finally got the better of him. The next thing I knew, he dropped the pistol, and I was standing over him, my shoes covered in bullet fragments, and my gun was smoking. My first run was exactly that quick. It was my very first time handling a rifle. For a minute, neither of us spoke. The fact is that I was a follower. Although you have no say over the result when you're a follower, I never intended to kill anyone.

That served as the catalyst and basis for my friendship with Rick. Our discussions on life, leadership, and accountability deepened as my release date approached. One day, I told him that he occasionally reminded me of my parents—or rather, what I believed our conversations could have been if I had had the chance to meet him. Despite being a guy of few words, Rick always seemed to have a loaded question ready to ask. "Slim, I hear you. I'm merely making an effort to make amends, but I have a question for you: When was the last time you made a phone call to your mother to express your affection for her? The silence was terrible.

Make her a call. Express your affection for your mother. I reclined and observed my naive resistance. "You really do adore her, don't you?" Rick leaned closer to ask.

"Yes, of course I do, dude."

"However..."

"But, nothing, we're alright."

"You know, Slim, a lot of us vent our hurt on the ones who matter most to us. Sometimes, we are so similar to them and their methods that we are unaware of the hatred we may harbour for them. When we are unhappy with the person we have allowed ourselves to become, it can be difficult to accept the reflection of ourselves. But keep in mind that, given the materials we are made of and our backgrounds, we are all just trying our best. If we refuse to accept forgiveness for the transgressions of our own friends and family, then for whom are we to pray?

That was the last thing I spoke with Rick before he was moved to a different facility a few days before I was released. I was fine with it if those were the last things he ever said to me since they were the most significant and lasting words he had ever said, and they came at the exact moment I needed them. I left that table with the newfound mental tools I needed to view things differently. It took me a few plays through our conversation before I worked up the nerve to pronounce those three quite complicated phrases. I had expressed my love to my mother numerous times, but this time it would be a conscious decision, not just something you say as you head out the door or end a call. A routine took on new significance for me since I learned about aspects of my life that I was previously unaware of.

There was no better time to begin my new life's journey. My only choice was to get off to a good start because I would soon be returning home. I anxiously awaited my scheduled fifteen-minute call. I listened in to hear the guys who were using their phones before me discuss their calls with loved ones. One man was obviously talking to his wife on the phone because he used the terms "baby," "honey," and "sweetheart" every other line. He gave me a finger gesture to give him a few more minutes when he saw that I was leaning in. "All right, sweetie, some other people are waiting to call. I love you more, and I'll give you a call on Sunday. "The phone is all yours," he said, nodding, and hanging up after wiping it with his shirt.

Keeping things polite meant using whatever you had on hand to clean the phone, be it a shirt, rag, or napkin. He might have believed I was pressuring him for phone time because I was leaning in so closely. I was merely asking for an illustration of a man's vulnerability and confidence. As I cautiously entered my code, I heard the person next to me talking on the phone. Alright, Mom. I'll see you when I visit. I also love you. The woman on the other end of the line started the conversation, and I observed that both calls concluded with love. I was aware that this time, it would not be the case for me.

Click one more. While waiting for the automated voice to indicate that someone had replied, the prisoner phones clicked.

When it came time to register my name, I said, "You have a collect call from Wallace, your son"—beep. "From SCI Dallas State Prison, this call is being made. Click the "pound" symbol to answer this call. Beep. She responded.

Hey Mom, how are you doing? I said in a positive way.

"What is the issue, Wallace? She asked straight out of the gate, "You okay?"

Yes, but why?

"You sound funny, like something's wrong, I don't know."

I wasn't sure if she was just programmed to brace herself for the worst-case situation, or if she could sense when something wasn't right or odd about me as quickly as she usually could. I suppose it might set off some bells to be reminded every time we chat by a robotic voice that I am calling from a fucking prison.

"I'm alright. When I am home in a few days, you can watch what I do.

"Oh, I see. Alright, Wally, that makes sense. You wouldn't believe how much they're marking up this food—I just got back from the grocery. In an attempt to increase sales, I had to visit two or three different stores.

Anger, bitterness, and negligence began to bubble beneath the surface of my tightening chest. Like a train pulling out of its station, my mother could not stop talking about her week. She never stopped to inquire about my plans. She never gave me more than a moment to consider what I should do next. As usual, it ached. Her speech reduced to a single buzz of incomprehensible phrases. My raging emotions were engulfed by Rick's final words to me, and I remembered him assuring me that she was only trying her hardest. Perhaps she was scared of being let down by more deceptive expectations and assurances. Maybe she wouldn't allow anyone to trespass into her heart and damage her if she shut me and everyone else out and made it appear like it was all about her. My eyes filled with tears, reflecting pieces of herself in me.

She said, "Well, okay, Wally, it was good talking to you," even though I had barely said anything during the ten minutes that had gone by.

Beep!"You're down to one minute left," the tape said. It was either now or never.

"Mom."

"What?"

"I cherish you."

I came to the realisation that silences say more than words ever could for the first time in my life.

"Okay, I also love you."

There were only a few seconds remaining, so we both took a moment to breathe out. Without saying goodbye, I hung up. My heart was still thumping loudly in my throat. I realised we both needed a lot of self-improvement.

NOW AT LAST, THE DAY WAS HERE. The jail crew was loading me into the prison transport van so they could send me off at the Greyhound station in Scranton, Pennsylvania. I'm sure you're wondering how things were going before I left. I could assure you that there will be no send-off celebration, no heartfelt embraces or daps, no mementos to take home, and none of that. It's just as incredibly uncomfortable and filled with doubt as the day you're brought in for the first time. Men's jealousy is hidden behind smiles when they wish you would never board the bus or, worse, when they hope you are taken back in.

Luckily, I no longer had to deal with those issues. The brief van ride to the station ended with the first door to my freedom being opened.

That's all there is to it. You should stop here. As the transport officer came down the aisle, uncuffing the three of us and letting us go, the driver sarcastically muttered, "See you next month." That served as our trial run. I've heard of instances where men attacked an officer who was making fun of them and harassing them before the bus even arrived, and they were detained. Some people simply don't know what they would do in the absence of the institutional restraints. not me, though. Nothing could stand in the way of my favourite woman, Freedom, and me on the day I'd dreamed of.

I didn't need to use the quarters that the pay phones in the bus terminal required to make a phone call. A porter, an elderly man, came up to me with a jingling change in his pocket and gave me fifty cents. "Here ya go, man," he exclaimed.

"I'm grateful. How did you find out? Feeling a little ashamed, I said.

He smiled and said, "I've seen fellas come and go; just make sure you make this one your last go."

"I promise you, never again."

Instead of clicking with an automatic system, I listened enthusiastically as the phone rang after I went to that pay phone and inserted a quarter into the slot.

Steven said, "Yo," taking up the phone.

"Dog, meet me at the station in downtown Philadelphia in three hours. I will return home.

October 2001 was the month.

CHAPTER 12
HALFWAY HOUSE

AFTER AVAILABILITY At SCI Dallas, where twenty percent of the guys are there for life, I felt better than James Brown wearing a brand-new pair of patent leather shoes just after I said my first words. After being released to a halfway home, my main priority was to avoid going to prison, which meant staying away from DeDe, my girlfriend at the time. Her childhood acquaintance from the area, Thirteenth and Allegheny, was only around the corner. She visited me, sent money, and wrote me letters for nearly a year before my release.

There was a rule at the halfway house that required people to stay inside for a predetermined amount of days before being allowed to leave. It wasn't causing me any trouble. When I was finally allowed to leave, my Nanny's crib was only fifteen minutes away thanks to the visits from people from all across the route who brought me food and clothing. DeDe, though, was the primary. I started dating DeDe seriously when I was living halfway home.

Midway through June, while I was still living at the halfway house, DeDe dropped down a copy of Russell Simmons' book Life and Def: Sex, Drugs, Money, + God. I was genuinely committed to altering the course of my life at the time, and I saw music as a respectable means of leaving the streets. Simmons's tale inspired me at the time since I had very few concrete models for what this change meant.

DeDe called me after I dropped off the book, and I thanked her for the gift.

"I cherish you."

"We also adore you."

I took the phone away from my face.

Who the hell are we?

As I brought the receiver back to my face, I could hear DeDe laughing merrily.

"Who the hell are we?"

"Crazy, the other one I'm carrying."

The thrill of learning I would be a father was quickly eclipsed by fear, and I wish I could recall my reaction to DeDe at that very moment. Here I was, poised to become a father, just twenty-three years old, having spent nearly half of my life in and out of juvenile and adult jail centres. Being a father at the time and providing a child with the love and direction that I lacked would have made me the happiest person alive. But my heart constricted when I considered what I could provide. Since I haven't even come to terms with what it means to be better than me, how could I ever educate a child to do the same? I partially contemplated the idea of becoming a father at that very moment, even though I would later persuade DeDe that it wasn't the best option. I also assumed that my aspirations of becoming a rapper would have to wait in favour of earning money as quickly as possible.

Even though I didn't let myself grieve for the unborn child at the time, realising that I was already following in my father's footsteps and that my child would eventually follow in mine devastated me more than anything. Although I took great pride in the legends and myths I knew about my father, I would exchange them all for the guy himself. I wasn't ready to cope with the sorrow of knowing that there is no greater legacy for a child than being present, and that I wasn't in a position in my life to ensure my own presence in my child's life.

A few weeks later, I went out rolling dice with the guys. Along with the mixtapes, I was touring and selling T-shirts with some of the members of Major Figgas, the rap group I founded. I reasoned that I could gather some extra ends. That was not the case. I went in expecting to use the dice to bust heads, but I ended up getting busted in the head. In an attempt to reverse my fate as soon as it was sealed, I tried to take advantage of the slow development of my rapping career, the impending birth of a child, and my stubborn attitude at the time. I thought the heist would help me make up for the dice game loss, but I lost much more in the end.

CHAPTER 13
GOING TO HOLLYWOOD

"Go, go, go!" I yelled as I dashed back to Mikey's 1997 green Yukon, climbed into the passenger seat, and ducked under. Mikey put his foot down on the gas before I could even close the door. The tires squealed as he pulled off into Carlisle Street, leaving a burnt rubber odour in our wake. Already sprawled out on the back seat,

Steven kept saying, "What happened, dog? Have you taken anything? "Dude, just let's return to the crib!"

Before we parked, we made a lap around Mikey's house to make sure no one was following. We parked the vehicle roughly half a street away, in case something happened, but the coast was clear. I glanced out the four windows back and forth, paranoid.

"Dude, what happened? Mikey insisted, "You were just supposed to go in there and check out the scene."

"Yeah, but as soon as I walked in, they started observing me intently."

"They?" What then transpired? What were you given? Seated almost in my face, Steven questioned from the rear seat.

"Dude, I went in and took a quick look around; the girl was at the register just as you had said." I paused to cover my face with my red scarf and recline in my seat. "Fuck it, this shit looks sweet; let me just tuck my hand under my shirt and make the jawn think I had a piece on me and have her clear out the cash drawer," I murmured. I could still feel Mikey and Steven's eyes burning a hole in me even with my eyes closed, waiting for me to tell them exactly how everything went and how much we gathered.

"So, what's going on? What were you given? Steven pleaded.

"Please wait until I finish. Just as I was ready to approach the short guy at the register, this burly dude emerged from the rear. I was thinking, Whoa, I didn't realise the homegirl was working the store by herself. I immediately left because I could tell they were going to call them boys on me—man, that guy was diesel and was assessing me."

There was an overwhelming hush in the car. I took off my scarf in order to read their reactions and finish telling them lies convincingly because it was so silent. Although Mikey never brought him up, there was another employee in there who wasn't even larger than I was. He wasn't at all buff. To be honest, he was genuinely attempting to help me obtain the DVD I requested, but that wouldn't support my argument to the guys. Ultimately, I couldn't bear the thought of serving another sentence in prison for the same error. I had already spent the previous five years in and out of jail. Steven and Mikey erupted into fits of giggles.

"Yooo! Regarding whom are you speaking to? The diminutive, slender man with the misaligned hairline? Mikey laughed and let out a cry.

How on earth did he know?

"Dude, I have no idea about any of that. All I knew was that he seemed to have Five-O on speed dial when he appeared out of nowhere, and I had no desire to hang around and find out. Furthermore, you mentioned that there should have only been one female employee. It's possible that I became stuck. The jokes and snark that I lost the ball on something that should have been as simple as pie continued from Mikey and Steven. The fact that I was being called every moniker in the book didn't phase me for one second. It was me who had spent almost the entire five years in prison; it was much better to get roasted by my boys than to be in constant fear of being shanked in your sleep. It was all games and fun, clowning and snapping, until Mikey left without a word.

"Stop! Now, where are we heading? I stood up to ask, but Mikey didn't bother to respond as he continued driving. He glanced into the rearview mirror and saw Steven again.

"Give the hammer to me." I understand this. Wallo, you have to quit playing," Steven continued. "That baby isn't going to feed itself, I told you."

I turned to face Stevie again, remembering how I'd just told him about DeDe and the baby, and now the secret information was being used to convince me to do something more that would put me in danger of going to jail again. I reached behind and took Steven's gun as Mikey drove up in front of the Blockbuster. I didn't have it in me to disappoint anyone, not even myself. Not at this moment. Its handle's cold metal shot a chill down my spine.

"I can do this! Come on, Stevie! Mikey, keep the truck in drive and stay focused!

Although the two guys were surprised, I couldn't take the chance that they would enter the room, drop the ball, and then have to deal with the fallout. I foolishly believed that the only way to reduce the danger would be to walk in and get it done myself. Like I used to, but a little quicker and smarter this time. I had a deep-seated conviction that after taking this final road, I would never again fall victim to anything similar. Exiting the truck, I tucked the SIG Pro.357 beneath my white T-shirt.

"Hey. You know that Denzel film that was released a few years ago?
I inquired with the trim cat from before.
"I believe that is Remember the Titans,"
Indeed.
"That's right over here, okay?" I rammed the rifle into his back as
soon as he turned to take the DVD down from the shelf. "Remain
calm, and I won't harm you." I urgently need everything entered into
the register. I moved Steven back toward the counter, watching him
carefully from the entrance. I gave the girl at the register a shake of
my head, telling her not to shout or move. More cash. Lower
yourself and open the safe. I require everything! And you, go back
there and bring me the tape from today's date," I yelled at the
terrified female. Play no! Straight back to the truck, we ran outside.
Just as I had predicted, Mikey took off. I could tell we didn't have
more than a thousand dollars based on the weight of the money.
What actually mattered, though, was that I had the surveillance tape.
We drove quickly, veering left on Carlisle, right on St. Luke, and
then left again on Broad Street, reaching Cayuga. I experienced a
surge of energy. We got away, not because I was happy to be back
on route. That was it! the final one. Never once more. Whipping and
spinning through Philadelphia's back streets, I was content knowing
that I was checking out of the game, until the sound of police sirens
blaring came from behind us. "Oh my god. Go, go, go!
We had to run down the block on foot after the truck crashed into a
row of parked automobiles, which happened in a matter of two or
three minutes at most. Right then, it was every guy for himself.
Stevie must have moved away from me because I was no longer able
to see him in my peripheral vision. There were cops everywhere. A
woman we saw standing on her porch was home when Mikey and I
ran into her house, and she yelled at us to leave. I pleaded with her to
keep silent. All we have to do is keep quiet for a bit. But she shrieked
the moment the police cars sped down her block. "They are in my
home right now!"
Mikey took off upstairs, and I hurried to the rear, breaking the poor
woman's cabinet off the wall and stealing her window screen before
sprinting across her lawn. However, it was already too late. I leaped
forward in front of a cop who was staring at my face with his
revolver pulled. Behind me, the sound of the handcuffs clicking was
like a kick to the stomach. Down the alleyway, I could hear the

woman screaming inside. All three of us were made to sit on the curb in front of a growing throng by the officers while we were being led around the corner. At that point, I knew Mikey had also been apprehended, but I wasn't sure about Stevie. It was after an hour or so that we were recognized as the robbers by Blockbuster witnesses who were brought to the scene. Bags of cocaine and rounds of ammunition that had been taken from Mikey's truck were being examined by police officials as they rummaged through them. B*tch. It didn't matter that I was unaware that those were included. It was all of ours in the eyes of the law. I would also be the one to suffer the most consequences. It was only nine months since I was released from prison.

CHAPTER 14
TIME IS MONEY

That person who said that crime doesn't pay wasn't lying at all. In 2002, the minimum wage in Philadelphia was $5.15 per hour at the time of our arrest. We split the $859 the day Mikey, Stevie, and I were apprehended for that Hollywood heist. That works out to $286 for each person. A wage worker would need to put in 55 and a half hours of work in order to earn as much as we did for ten minutes of labour. For a dishonest day's work, quite excellent. That is, if we managed to escape. We didn't.

For $286, I served for fifteen years. Let's calculate that. You would receive two thousand hours if we took a forty-hour full-time schedule and multiplied it by fifty weeks each year (vacation included). Thirty thousand hours are obtained by multiplying two thousand by fifteen, which is the amount of years I served. I earned $0.009 per hour after dividing the $286 by the thirty thousand hours I was incarcerated. Less than a fucking dime, really. While crime may seem profitable at first, the long-term costs are much higher.

The condition of receiving the duration I did is that you have to be appreciative. This is the reason why: I was convicted of my first major crime in 1996—the heist at Kentucky Fried Chicken. I was seventeen at the time, and I had been so accustomed to using the juvenile system that I assumed I might spend the same amount of time there.

However, jail and prison are not the same thing. Before you are successfully tried and found guilty of a crime, you are sent to jail. Once convicted and given a sentence, you are sent to prison. If liberty is paradise, then confinement is purgatory and hell. I was therefore in the wing for the young children who had received adult certification. Someone was being condemned every day I was there, and listen, buddy, I remember this one day a guy came back with his life. Another guy made twenty to forty. I remember crying and simply putting my towel up in my cell one day because I couldn't fathom living off the streets at that point. I told myself, "Man, I could do six, I could do five, but I just can't handle all of this."

I had a lot on my mind when it came time for the armed robbery, thus. I felt twenty percent gratitude, twenty percent melancholy, and sixty percent deathly afraid. I was grateful since everyone else—the majority of the guys returning from court—had been given far more time than that. Subsequently, I was listening to these younger guys my own age who consider themselves experts and practice jailhouse law.

"Yeah, they're probably going to give you twelve and a half to twenty-five." Black people in this nation are treated so poorly that we make an effort to seem as though suffering is not real. So, as I rode the bus from the courthouse back to the jail, I readied myself. I was getting ready as if I would never walk on the block.

"They granted me twenty-seven years, so it's not nothing at all," I remarked.

I was giving out the back number to others as I was leaving. I entered my cell and began attempting to understand this stupid fear. This is really happening.

CHAPTER 15
MRS. OFFICER

Five years into my sentence, this new female C.O. approached me while I was strolling around the track in the yard. She said that her cousin, a neighbouring friend, had told her that I was here and asked her to come talk to her. You notice kindness in prison because it's uncommon. And as soon as I noticed it, I saw that this C.O. was attractive, with a five-six stout frame and skin the colour of Starbucks caramel coffee. I decided to repay her courtesy by being amiable and explaining how the prison operated, as well as what to watch out for and which other convicts to avoid. A deed for another deed.

We had those conversations for a few weeks until she stopped me when we were in the yard.

"I'll give you this address so you can send me letters."

She just gave me the address. I immediately committed it to memory and tossed away the paper since I didn't want to ruin either of our spots. Having spent so many years in prison, I had a lot of experience composing love letters. So I wrote her a very casual first letter. I was just exchanging innocent thoughts of desire with her, like a teenage girl in puppy love—how lovely I thought she was, how I wish I could take her out to dinner at her favourite restaurant, all the kind of stuff you could read in a Terry McMillan novel. First, I was keeping the true gentleman.

She appeared more anxious to get past the niceties and hear my true intentions when I emailed her back. All I needed to hear was that. I went and wrote Zane a jealousy-inspiring letter full of cold blood. "Imagine This" is the title of the letter I wrote.

IMAGINE THIS...
It's the middle of the night and you opened my cell up. You came into the cell and as though you knew we didn't have a lot of time, I kissed you immediately. You took your uniform off. After you took the uniform off, I put you on your knees and you showed me how your lips felt. Then I put you over the bed and returned the favour, pleasuring you from the back until you woke the entire prison up...

After reading the letter, she got in touch with me again and remarked, "Every time I see you, my body melts." She was attracted to me because I could make her curious. It's not necessary to go to jail to learn this lesson, and I'm not advocating for being a prisoner either, but as guys, we have all the resources at our disposal—money, jewels, and elegant dates—to draw in women when we're not incarcerated. But when you are imprisoned, all you have are your thoughts and the ability to create a vision that needs to appear as real as the outside world. She eventually turned into one of the guards that came to watch over me that day when I was downstairs in the kitchen, a few weeks later. Being one of the top chefs at the establishment, I was given a lot of leeway and self-assurance. I walked to one of the shelves near her and pretended to be looking for something before whispering to her about one of the prison's blind spots while my man Psycho was relaxing down there. Because this was an old institution, there were many blind spots that the cameras were unable to capture. Many of us honed our skills in the grey areas, learning to see in areas the cameras couldn't. People will usually support you. The technique known as stemming involves having a reliable prisoner create a distraction so you can finish tasks before anyone notices. So I followed her to a storage room and she did the stemming for me. She went in first, and I trailed in behind her, acting as though I was looking for something. I moved in, grabbed her behind, and gave her a quick kiss. I'm gripping her neck and thrusting my tongue between her lips. Even if it's great to physically touch a soft lady, nothing was more essential to me than her employment stability. I didn't want us to be found out for this reason. I had to stop her from getting up to speed. Two minutes in this seductive storage closet developed into what seemed like an endless kiss.

When I run into her again in the yard a few days later while she's working her shift, she tells me she has a cell phone number for me that isn't under her name.

I asked, "What do you mean?"

"The days I work here are not enough. I have to talk to you about this right now.

I entered the number to my phone list, which is a list of all the people you can call who have to be authorised by the prison. For individuals who may be wondering, "Surely the jail would keep an eye on the calls?" That's not at all what you see on television. Perhaps if you're a well-known drug dealer or kingpin, but for the average prisoner, after what seems like some boo-loving, there's really no need to go too personal. You have to take into account the financial resources that the state would need in order to have correctional guards watch thousands of prisoners' conversations. It's just not realistic. For the next month, we talked on the phone about things like where I would take her after I got out, what we would do if we had more time, and what kind of sexual things I would do to her the next time I saw her. She would just say, "I can't wait till you come home," to me. "Come home" was our code for that storage closet, and we were talking about how we would have more time than ever to have sex while we were behind bars. By the time I saw her again, I was starting to feel like that Ready for the World song, "Love You Down". I felt totally comfortable. On the day I showed up for my kitchen job, Psycho was already waiting for me in the closet. As soon as I went through the door, she unfastened her belt, shoved her jeans down to her ankles like they were on fire, and hunched over the boxes. She felt like a fucking bag of nickels as I slid inside her like I was at a water park. I felt like I had five and a half strokes of freedom. In the two years that we were together, we may have had sex four times. But we persevered because of how strong those times were. But one day, her enthusiasm faded. She was no longer replying to my emails or returning my calls. When we saw each other, we would always find a way to come close to each other, unlike before when she seemed to be always out of reach. I couldn't quite put my finger on it, but I knew she had to be communicating with someone else. Regardless of what I gave her while she was here, at the end of the day, she could go where I couldn't, which was out this motherfucker.

CHAPTER 16
REFLECTION POINTS

Time has the ability to subdue the beast within you. With enough time, one can soothe even the most voracious of appetites. For me, the complex web of deception I clung to has been gradually dismantled by time. Time replaced my haughtiness with responsibility, and it became my silent teacher. It may sound strange, but after a little while I understood that the purpose of my second stint in prison was to give me more time to develop into the guy I had begun to become just before my early release. I was not mentally prepared to be a man on my own in the outside world, putting the lessons I had learned from my first stint in prison to use. I hate to say this. But it took patience and humility for me to realise that.

The day I discovered the word ravenous is still fresh in my memory; it was among the first terms my cursor fell upon when I aimlessly leafed through the dictionary pages in the legal department of the library, hoping to expand my vocabulary. One of the things the wise people would always tell me to do is to thumb through law books and dictionaries. During my prison sentence, I made a self-imposed pledge to myself that I would enhance my vocabulary. Finding three words that start with the same letter and starting to use them in everyday speech was one of the challenges. The other two terms that seemed to leap off the pages and demand my attention were reflect and redeem.

This little task pushed me to apply the term reflect in my life and make it work for me in some way, rather than just in conversation. I considered what it meant to look back on my life with candour; it was the first time I had ever seen my real self in the mirror. I gave myself permission to consider the areas of my life that I had spent the most of my time ignoring. I had never seen such filthy layers festering inside of me. I had no idea I was harbouring years' worth of unresolved resentment, hatred, and self-righteous victimisation; they were building inside of me like a volcano ready to blow.

It was the first time in my life when my self-destructive and illogical denial had no mask to hide behind. There was no mask left to take my mind off the suffering and agony I brought onto others. I was under the mistaken impression that my good intentions could excuse me from committing horrible things, therefore I committed careless crimes. I had a ton of justifications for why what I was doing on those streets wasn't as horrible as everyone was making it seem. Oh, I'm quite giving. I'm good because I give back the majority of my earnings to the hood. Yes, I promised myself that I would never shoot anyone. I'm looting multimillion dollar companies, not them directly. Oh, and I didn't damage anyone when I did jack someone directly; it was simple and quick.

I covered up my wrongdoings for years, using any excuses I could think of to justify my actions. I pretended to be a follower while taking the initiative wherever I went. I did not consider for a moment how traumatising it could have been for the ladies and men, young and old, that I was pointing weapons at. The thought that I could have killed myself or someone else struck me like a ton of bricks the instant I gave myself permission to reflect on myself in depth.

Maturity and growth were not acquired quickly or readily. Removing the layers of the careless tyrant I'd allowed myself to become was an arduous and difficult task. Amidst the everyday mayhem and madness that occurred within the enclosed hell known as a prison cell, there was nowhere to turn or anybody to turn to. The rehabilitation of career criminals would simply jeopardise the job security of officers and personnel, who solely had an interest in their own careers. I had to work by myself on this.

CHAPTER 17
THE BOOK OF LIFE

I was in the worst emotional and mental state I had ever been when I returned from my trial. I was an angry, flaming ball of fire. I was filled with fury and angry at the world. I probably wouldn't have survived there if the judge had been able to extend my sentence by years because of how I lost it after learning that I was found guilty.

"I'll see you once more." Just like the renowned California governor declares, "I'll be back," As the cops hauled me back to my harsh world, screaming and swearing, I screamed at the judge. It took me a few years of bitterness and rage before I could truly accept who I was. I have to extend forgiveness to everyone. Above all, I needed to learn how to forgive myself.

I was solely concerned with not wanting to go back to prison for the first six years of my bid. I knew that this time, in 2008, I was done. I will always remember: It was July, and the summer heat was as intense as that of a Toyota's hood. Not only was the air heated in prison because there was no air conditioning, but it also smelled strongly of musty, sweaty grown men. It was all in the yard, but I made up my mind that I wanted to be by myself.

I went to my cell's faucet and sprayed water on my face in an attempt to remain calm. The notion struck me like a sock full of Dial soap bars while I was staring at myself in the mirror: What the fuck is wrong with me? I am incarcerated due to my false identity. For I had a conscience, even when I was stealing and boosting. I was aware that what I was doing was wrong, but I was too scared to face the fact that I would need to make changes and I was at a loss as to how. Life has a way of lifting you up when you're at your lowest point, and that's how I got into watching Anthony Bourdain.

We were allowed to use our commissary funds to purchase televisions and cable subscriptions while we were incarcerated. In order to watch TV in our cells without disturbing our fellow prisoners, we also needed to purchase headphones. When I got a television and decided it was time to alter my ways, the Travel Channel quickly became one of my favourite channels to watch because it offered the only means of getting me out of prison. I travelled the world with the television series Parts Unknown, The

Layover, and No Reservations. I saw several regions of the nation, as well as the top eateries, beaches, and tourist attractions, thanks to The Travel Channel. I watched so many episodes that I can't even remember which ones I watched because they all seemed like one big movie. Seeing the world outside of North Philadelphia and the prison walls, however, had a positive overall impact.

Out of all the things I do recall learning about particular episodes of the series, the one that affected me the most was discovering that Anthony Bourdain was getting stoned in New York City prior to being this renowned chef who travelled the world. It opened my eyes to the limitless possibilities, which positively transformed me. Being members of our communities, we occasionally have restricted role models. Prior to learning about Bourdain's background, I concentrated on the differences between us. I assumed his life was simple because he was a white man and didn't seem to be from the same world as myself. Then I found out about his battles with addiction and saw that he never seemed to think he was superior to anyone, regardless of who he spoke to. He had the same level of curiosity about common people as he had about diplomats. From Bourdain's broadcasts, I discovered that people who were good with people and words had a future, regardless of their history. This made me realise that I could make friends with anyone and talk to people from all backgrounds.

During my bid, I also developed a fascination for advertising, which was the show. I would simply switch on the TV and wait for the commercials to end. When I saw the way the patties were arranged on the bun in a McDonald's commercial, the lettuce was crisp, and the bun was all gooey, and I remember thinking, "My burger never looked like that." For some reason, that advertisement motivated me to learn more about the marketing industry, even though I knew at the time that this had nothing to do with marketing. And George Lois's Damn Good Advice (For People with Talent!): How to Unleash Your Creative Potential by America's Master Communicator was one of the best books I ever read when I was incarcerated.

Lois, the author of several of the most successful marketing campaigns in history, explains these insights into the workings of advertising and marketing in her book. "A Big Idea Can Change World Culture" is among the ideas that I can still clearly recall the most. According to Lois, a Big Idea was an effort to convey a brand by crafting a powerful message that went against the conventions of the company and connected with the target audience. The hustlers in the neighbourhood were promoting and advertising their lives when I thought of how they would drive around in their Benz, playing loud music, flashing jewels, and displaying knots of $100 bills while the fine woman sat in the passenger seat. You can't draw people to your way of life by showing them everything, even when the reality of living on the streets comes with far more than diamonds and Dom Pérignon. It's imperative to present individuals with what you want them to see and what you know they desire to view.

I came to the realisation that a large portion of my own path was not shaped by the reality of the streets but rather by the way it was marketed to me when I thought back to the area where the hustlers were glorified and the nine-to-fivers were ignored. I realised after reading that book that everything businesses show us is a game. This piqued my interest more and took me farther down this informational rabbit hole. After that, I became aware of Steve Stoute, who at the time was the author of a book titled The Tanning of America: How Hip-Hop Created a Culture That Changed the New Economy's Rules. Because he was able to see the importance of Black culture and communicate that value to businesses so that our experiences would be represented more widely, Stoute is regarded as a respected member of the community. Ironically, Stoute was also the brains behind the creation of "Ba da ba ba bah, I'm lovin it," one of McDonald's most recognizable slogans. Anybody from the ghetto knows that as a hustler, the hustle never changes, even though it might be absurd to assume that a person who raps about drugs could write one of the most popular and memorable jingles for one of the biggest companies in the world.

I started to change my viewpoint and developed an entirely new way of thinking. I began to refocus and treat the remaining time I had in prison like it was Princeton. It was no longer entertaining, nor was it anything to worry about, what was going on in the yard and the chow halls. I turned my cell into a classroom where I could teach and be taught. I had a laser-like focus on becoming the man I yearned to be, while striving for flawless attendance. My past against my future, it was now or never.

My new writing style took precedence over my Letters to Freedom. I began writing daily narratives in a journal that I called "The Book of

Life." The narrative at first concerned what I was seeing around me. I purposefully chose the language I used, referring to the men as "men" rather than "inmates" or "prisoners." I wrote about a number of subjects, one of which was the harm that could result from prolonged seclusion in a hole and the psychosis it could induce, which could test the mettle of even the most resilient individuals. In my piece, I discussed the sleep deprivation brought on by guys who, driven by their own demons, would beat on steel toilet bowls like drums for hours on end or scream in a rage-fueled insanity till the sun rose.

After a few months of writing in my new format, I understood that the words on the paper in front of me were the very things I wanted to put far behind me. Although nothing could completely remove the eerie suffocation of spending years behind bars, I believed that writing about it would help me start the process of truly recovering.

"The Book of Life" was a set of instructions that helped me overcome my urge for change and changed me in ways I never would have thought possible. There were no principles or norms governing its organisation. All I had to do was write it all down and be really honest about my aims and worries. My mind became open to possibilities the instant I gave myself permission to know what I wanted out of life and how to get it. Without worrying about being judged or rejected, I was able to write openly about the objectives and concepts I wished to realise. For me, that was the big turning point in the game.

As I kept writing, I became aware that I was experiencing very intense feelings. One thing stood in the way of my transformation at every turn: my connection with my mother. She casually stated, "You'll be alright," when I called her following my sentencing, and I could still clearly recall her comments as if they were yesterday. I felt as though that wave of callous disdain would break every fibre in my body. Her remarks, along with the numbing sensation they evoked, remained frozen in time until I came to terms with the fact that my mother was also a victim of my past.

You do not enter prison by yourself. Not even the alone time is done by you. The people you love are actually emotionally suspended in a mental cell next to you. Your misdeeds and bad choices also victimise and penalise them, from the cost of hiring attorneys, posting bail, and maintaining a commissary to the stress of staying up late to attend court hearings.

I realised that for a few years, I had been clinging to that moment. I should have been learning how to be real in my apology for all the dysfunction I contributed to while I was learning how to forgive. I started to realise that her heart had to have grown cold because of the grief I'd given her. I understood that this was one of the wounds I would need to learn how to heal if I wanted to change.

Shoes, my roommate, gave me advice on a variety of perspectives on life. His viewpoints opened my eyes to new possibilities. Strangely enough, Shoes was an original who knew my father and could share helpful anecdotes about him. Shoes was an ill man, with disease and ageing spots on his hands. Occasionally, he would catch me glancing at them and would tremble his thinning hands, covering them with embarrassment. I used to push him around and listen to him because he had cancer and was in a wheelchair.

I would reassure him, telling him we were in a safe place, "Don't worry about that, OG; I'm just in the zone, listening," while he shared stories from his life. He progressively faded away from what we believed to be cancer while we lived in close quarters for a few years. He resembled a father figure in certain ways.

I'm confident that being bunkies with Shoes was a result of divine intervention, as everything happens for a reason. It gave me the confidence to sit through my flitting thoughts and get into my emotions to have an older brother who grew up in the same era as my father. If I had been partnered with someone even remotely as enraged and resentful as I was upon my reintroduction into the system, I could only imagine the chaos that would have ensued. The hellfire that once raged in my heart could have been ignited with little effort. I see now that I require love and love in return. There aren't many males in prison who would say those things to you. We dread vulnerability with all our hearts. But I would not have progressed this far if Shoes had not given me words of love, support, and advice. I discovered the true meaning of loss and love through him.

Shoes began to get ill over time and found himself spending more and more time in the hospital and nursing stations inside the prison. Bit by bit, my heart broke at the sight of his condition and the breaking of his once hopeful spirit. It was a two-edged blade; on the one hand, it let light into parts of my heart that had been closed off for a long time, waiting for my father to fill them.

During the day, I would pick him up from the hospital wing and take him outside to get some fresh air to help him manage his discomfort. Shoes eventually grew too weak and wanted to stay inside and take as much rest as possible. At that point, I began checking out additional library books to read aloud in our cell. My reading abilities were below average before, but this practice improved them. It also increased my awareness of my cadence and voice projection. I would eventually require these abilities as weapons in my toolbox to carry out the self-prophecies I had recorded in "The Book of Life."

Shoes adored these sugar-dusted candies known as orange slices. I used to buy him some every time I went to the commissary and spent my free time chatting to him. It resembled a connection between a parent and son the most. I was sitting next to him one day in 2005 when he grabbed my arm.

With a harsh tone, he said, "Listen man." "I need you to do me a favour when you go out."

"What should I do when I visit the yard?"

He shot out, "I'm not talking about no damn yard." "I'm referring to the time you return home."

"What?"

"I've been in and out of these joints my entire life. I have never witnessed anything. I'm not going anywhere. He held my arm like a death grip. "Enjoy your motherfucking existence." Please just complete it for me.

I said to Shoes, "I'm going to do it."

"You are unique, Wallo."

Even though I was grateful for what he was telling me, I couldn't help but feel that he was either insane or knew something that I was unaware of. When I'm serving a second prison sentence for breaking my pre-release, he was telling me that I'm different.

A nurse advised me to come back later or on a different day as I waited for a guard to get Shoes out of his hospital bed the following day. Shoes was one of the toughest guys I had ever met, so even though I knew something had to be wrong or that his agony had gotten worse, I chose to have faith in him.

"Miss, no issue at all. Tell him that I stopped by and that we have some excellent work to accomplish. We used to refer to our studies, journaling, and the sporadic deeds of kindness we pushed one another to accomplish as "good work."

That day, I was eager to sit with Shoes since I had finally obtained the "Purple Book." We gave Iyanla Vanzant's book its title because of its striking purple cover: Acts of Faith. If you had one of these books, it rapidly became one of the most traded books on the block and had a lengthy waiting list. Who was trying to better themselves might be discerned even at a distance by the literature they selected. The majority of men who weren't prepared for change read novels like America's Master Swindler and 48 Laws of Power by "Yellow Kid" Weil. Though fashionable, those volumes were also referred to as "con man's bibles."

One of the most influential novels I've ever read is "The Purple Book," so I was eager to begin reading it with Shoes. I thought we could utilise the inspiring messages and daily affirmations to help him get better day by day while he recovered. Before freedom came to look for us, it would have given us something to look forward to and kept us grounded as our hours changed into days and those days became years.

Later that day, I learned that Shoes had died the previous evening from problems related to HIV.

Many things are undone by grief. Among them is faith. I felt my faith quickly crumble beneath me upon hearing the awful news. The "good work" we had completed together began to seem pointless. Sadness turned into shock, then into bitterness, and, worst of all, into the loneliness of fatherhood concerns.

Shoes' final words, "You're special," served as my lifeline—a concrete object I could cling to while I struggled with the grief. I turned more to God than I ever had after I first lost religion. I asked for guidance and a restraining force to help me stay on course and carry on the excellent work we began. I prayed because Nanny had always told me that prayer is the only way to experience miracles. I combined Eastern spirituality, Islam, and Christianity in my prayers. I urgently needed a miracle.

A few weeks later, I got a call from an officer telling me that I had to be ready to make room in my cell for a new knucklehead cellmate because my time alone there was almost over. We had no idea that my brother Steven, who was serving his sentence in Pine Grove, had just arrived as a new cellmate.

Take a look at God!

I don't know if Steven moving to Dallas with me would qualify as a miracle, but God knew I needed something, or someone, to help me survive. That's one thing I could tell you. And the closest thing I had ever experienced to a miracle was probably seeing my brother's face after years in prison.

"Yeah!"

"Oh my god. Yeehaw!

Between the fits of laughing and bear hugging, those were the only words that came to mind. Regretfully, I had already been imprisoned alongside family members before. Only a few years prior, Hip, Jalal's father, had also shared a cell with me for a few months. It appeared as though my friends and relatives were welcomed with a welcome mat at the prison's revolving door.

While a lot had changed in the time I'd been gone, many bad things had persisted. Examples of these changes were cars, technology, and fashion. Steven's drug addiction continued to be the main factor in the crimes he did. Getting your paper together and getting it is the only way to scratch that itch when you need a fix. Sometimes, you might be able to obtain it on credit, and on other occasions, you might just get lucky on a route. Even with low cash, credit is still the worst alternative, as everyone knows. You typically end up repaying far more than you originally owed. I would constantly reflect back on that day a lot. Steve drove me there on the day my mother's foot was hurt. when he gave me a tour of the street gang. Every time I end up behind bars, I can't help but think back to that day. I reflect on how he exposed me to a life of crime and how, living on the streets, I was always losing bets with my life. My brother introduced me to the street game; why? That is what I would ask myself. But until I learned to accept responsibility for my own actions, that question made me resentful of Steven and occasionally furious with him.

Steven and I were closer than ever during the course of the following six months. We spoke late into the night about life, our early years, and all the concepts I had jotted down in the "Book of Life" that would eventually assist in ending the vicious cycle that our family was living. I don't think anyone in this world still has more faith in me than Steven does. He used to watch me read voraciously and pace the floor until an idea struck, at which point I would scramble to jot it down in my notebook.

"Boy, you're going to be large when you leave here this time! Really huge, I promise! Wallo, you have a mean hustle about you. Compared to the other niggas in this room, you have more hustle. I promise I can spot a star when I see one, even if you never paid attention to anything I had to say. stated Steven.

And I gave him credit for it.

CHAPTER 18
MOMENTUM

THINGS FOR Steven and ME STARTED TO LOOK UP. Together, we made the decision to participate in the prison addiction program so that I could support him and learn coping mechanisms for friends and family after I was released back into society. The thing about those kinds of programs is that anyone can benefit from them, even if they are not an addict. It makes sense to be open and honest about your flaws when you're in a group environment where nobody can criticise you. I explained that I was selling to people who were similar to them because of my previous addiction to quick money. I would see the stars on the faces of men who seemed to hate me for never having tried drugs but were still able to profit from their failure.

Being there every week for weeks on end gave me a goal. I discovered how to resolve issues with people I had unintentionally damaged indirectly by confronting them. I was able to confront the numerous traumas in my life and let go of some of the sadness I was still holding on to by communicating openly. This allowed me to gradually forgive myself for the mistakes I had made.

One specific young man named Rico was a part of the program, and it was evident that he was occasionally still mentally disturbed. He was clearly walking the edge of addiction. The other side had a solid grip on him, while the other wanted him to clean up and finish the program. Steven was perplexed as to why I was interested in Rico's recovery. Steven has always been, to be honest, a certified hater. For good cause, he detested everyone and everything that wasn't family. My brother would argue that his perception was shaped by trust difficulties, but that was also his method of making sure no one could take advantage of him. In less than 32 seconds, he could profile someone and call their bluff. That was another trick that a con guy learnt. He was honest and forthright in his speech, expressing his emotions as they came to him without regard for whether or not it offended you. Now that I think about it, when we were younger, he was the exact opposite of me since I tried my hardest to fit in with everyone.

Rico arrived at our class one day only a minute or two before we were locked out. Their rigorous punctuality policies had previously resulted in other men failing out of the program when they weren't followed. Rico was tall and lean, with a small moustache of dirt that reminded me of the one I had when I was first transferred to Dallas at the age of eighteen. I felt obliged to help because, in a way, he reminded me of my younger self. I gestured for him to take the vacant seat next to me, but he chose not to notice. The drug prevention counsellor began giving Rico papers with writing assignments on them as soon as he took a seat. When I turned to face Steven, he was already giving me a disgusted expression.

"Dude, you should take care of yourself!" Steven spoke in a gruff yet forceful voice.

I said, "Chill, he's cool," hoping to deter Steven from making a big deal. If you want to survive in prison, the most important guideline is to mind your own business and keep out of the way. My brother was merely attempting to protect me and prevent me from unintentionally taking on other people's burdens. Even making investments in the welfare of others can occasionally set you up for failure.Okay, peace, brothers. There have been some whispers that many of you are only here to gain points and possibly get some time cut when you go before the board, and that this program doesn't really offer any benefits. Now, while I can appreciate your desire to present the strongest case possible for your release when the time comes, I have to admit that hearing such negative feedback about our program depresses me. Depressing. Please write the word at the top of your worksheet if you are not familiar with it and search it up before next week. Like several of you, I have been in and out of jail for many years. I don't care how you feel about me; I'm serving my twenty-fifth year of a life sentence without the possibility of parole. However, I do care about your opinion of this program. Joe Brown stated, "I have devoted my entire life to this program and a few others, and getting approval for any of them hasn't been easy."

The designated drug program counsellor was Joe. He wore brown-tinted glasses to go with his skin and brown jumpsuit. We used to remark that his face, neck, and body were all one continuous shade, making it impossible to discern where they ended from a distance. I don't know if Brown was his last name or just a joke we made up.

Joe Brown removed his spectacles, something that not many people got to see. When the large goggle-like glasses quit enlarging his eyes, they nearly vanished. He wiped his wrinkled brow and beady, watery eyes before letting out a stressed-up groan.

"What do you know? I want to try something new today. I'll circle the group and give each of you a chance to speak to the man next to you, telling them how you feel about their development since the program began five weeks ago and how you hope they may improve before our sixth and last week together. Please, let's be civil and upbeat.

The news of the task caused the room to erupt in anxious laughter and sighs. A few men moved in their chairs, and one rubbed his hands tensely above his knees. Everybody except Rico responded.

"People, let's start with you."

"What?" I pointed to myself in response.

That's correct, Wallo. Let's begin with you. Kindly get up and begin with the person on your left.

I stood gingerly, trembling with my hands. "Well, Rico, let me start by saying thank you for coming to the meeting today."

The bunch burst out laughing right away.

"Guys, let him finish!" Joe reattached his Coke-bottle glasses and said. "Go ahead, people."

As I mentioned earlier, I appreciate your presence today. If I were to begin with a compliment, I would say that you have regularly attended the group, which must be taken into consideration.

Rico spoke up before me, whispering under his breath, "Dude, stop talking so much."

Once more, the group erupted into laughter.

"Nope, that's cool," I replied. "I could stop talking, but to be honest, it won't help either of us." Rico straightened his shoulders from his hunched position and met my gaze. "Look, you seem like you're wasting your time on your own, so I'm not going to waste anyone's time here—mine or yours." It was evident from the movement in the room that it caught everyone's attention and that they were prepared for a conflict of some kind.

Joe told them to keep going while he cleared the room.

"You remind me of myself when I was younger, and what's messing me up is that I didn't have my father around either, but the difference between you and me is that I don't have kids to stop that cycle for. I generally don't say stuff like this. Yes, you do! I was confined here once more, and I lost my blessing. With all due respect, I've heard you talk about your past and the man you were before doing drugs, so why are you still hanging onto that? Who cares what it was, really? Nothing mattered anymore—not your woman back home, not your kids. That was then! It's finished! How are you going to improve as a guy today? be a father who is sober? Because no one really cares about the person you used to be. Rico is no longer there! For a brighter tomorrow, who will you be today?

With each syllable, my voice's bass and words' strength increased. There was silence in the room. Not only was I speaking from the bottom of my heart for Rico, but also for Steven, to whom I would never have dared to voice these words.

"Whoa! Joe said, "Thank you, everyone, as I sat down and wiped a tear from my eye.

Indeed. And that is exactly how it is! I came to an end. Everyone laughed once more, letting go of the uneasy tension that comes with vulnerability.

That marked a turning point in my life. I realised then and there what my role was on this planet. I understood that while I would never be able to make up for the wrongs I had done in the past, I could still change the lives I touched going forward. I had an inside spark of energy that I had never experienced before.

"And it's just like that" became my go-to conclusion whenever I felt like it.

After the Board of Prisons advised After sending Steven to a rigorous six-month criminal rehabilitation program, we were split up into different blocks and couldn't see each other for a while. I used that time to attend many programs and earn multiple certificates. Among them, anger management caught my attention the most. Cognitive behaviour therapy and de-escalation techniques taught us how to avoid unnecessary and explosive confrontations; these are fancy terms for knowing when and how to talk yourself down from the brink before you punch someone in the face. As I continued to attend classes, I started to see myself as someone who could assist with rehabilitation and reform both inside and outside of prisons.

People that are depressed typically don't do anything. They merely sob at their circumstances. However, they make changes when they become enraged. I read that to the group; it's one of my favourite phrases from Malcolm X. I wanted them to know that while it's acceptable to be furious, what really counts is how you choose to channel your rage.

Steven and I were able to reunite in the yard over time. He was in the midst of having his case appealed after completing his program with success. As we sat and spoke about our future goals, we would bring various delicacies and snacks to share with one other.

"The people adore you, Lo, but I'm not sure what it is about you. You truly possess something unique. Oh no, I wish my attorney could also get you out of here. However, I swear, I will inform everyone back home about your moving here. He exclaimed, "I'm proud of you!" with enthusiasm in his voice. When we both returned to freedom, I was overjoyed to see my brother sober, ambitious, and prepared to assist me in taking over the world.

I would have clung to my brother more if I had known that day in the yard would be my last one.

A few days later, Steve's attorney won an appeal and had his guilty conviction reversed, allowing him to return home.

When your brother, your right hand, is given another shot at freedom but is forced to stay behind until your turn comes, you experience a range of emotions. Naturally, you're pleased for him and thrilled that at least one of you is out of the system, but you also have to deal with the sadness of losing him while you're still in the system. It could be difficult to navigate your emotions. It appears as though you have to let go of the chance to communicate those emotions before you can really absorb and comprehend them.

Even after reading numerous books and engaging in various programs, I lacked the necessary tools to identify my self-centred actions. Steven and I had a communication breakdown that lasted longer than it should have shortly after he moved back home. even years.

I was self-centred enough to believe Steven should go above and beyond to rescue me as well. I required $5,000 to hire a lawyer to assist me in my case appeal, just like he had needed for his counsel. He believed that my case would be unjustified and that paying legal fees would be unnecessary. Furthermore, it seemed to me that he opted to stay out of my legal dispute. I was here because he introduced me to the street game when I was younger, so his absence in this fight felt like a betrayal. Decades had passed since that introduction to the streets, so "unaccountable" may as well have been my middle name, yet I still wanted to hold someone else accountable for my own transgressions.

There wasn't much more I could accomplish without outside assistance than to use my imprisonment as a springboard for more prospects. In the midst of steel bars, I discovered my silver lining and became passionate about creating exquisite meals using the most basic ingredients. As word spread that I was the greatest cook when it came to potatoes, onions, and a few "borrowed" secret seasonings, I was promoted to Graterford Penitentiary in 2009. I like to exaggerate things sometimes, like what I just said. To tell the truth, I was alright. While working at the Dallas night bake shop, I stumbled upon Jeff Henderson's book Cooked, sometimes known as Chef Jeff. After reading his book, I became motivated to start learning more about cooking because, similar to me, he had worked in the prison kitchen before emerging as one of the best chefs in history. I shared this book with my counsellor after reading it because it greatly impressed me. I told my counsellor that I wanted to be just like Chef Jeff, so he put in for a promotion. I was prepared for a new notch on my belt that may change the game, even if Graterford was another maximum-security jail that I would have to navigate. Besides, they had a culinary arts program.

You notify your people when a transfer occurs, and this initiates a communication network whereby those in your social circle who know someone at the jail to which you are being transferred notify one another in advance of your arrival so they can be on the lookout for you upon your arrival. I reconnected with my former head, Big Jake, in this way. Jake was a tough guy with an Arnold Schwarzenegger-like build. We connected because the mother of his son and my mother got along well.

I entered Graterford's culinary program upon arrival, completed it, and was hired to prepare meals for 5,000 prisoners. I was able to make special meals for the kitchen staff in my free time because of my position in the kitchen. I created this side gig where I would sell platters of baked chicken, baked macaroni, fried fish, and fried rice for $10 for a pack of cigarettes. Big Jake started coming in for business. Big Jake was another wise guy who looked out for me for two years. He kept an eye on me, made sure I didn't fly too close to the sun, and kept me from drowning.

I spoke with my mother on the phone one day.

She said, "Wally, I have a story about Big Jake to tell you."

At this point, my mother revealed to me that she had dated Big Jake's brother prior to her and my father starting a relationship.

"One day, as your father and I were driving, Big Jake's brother and some of his friends were standing on the corner, and Big Jake opened fire on our vehicle." "Yeah, I was pregnant with you at the time," I said in shock.

How the hell about it?

I was processing at the time that I almost didn't have a life because of this old man who was educating me about it. I didn't have the intention of hurting Big Jake, even though my desire to do so was impetuous. I had no intention of disabling the brotherhood due to an incident that occurred in 1978. I started to believe Shoes when he stated that I was unique at that very moment.

I continued to put the same level of emphasis on my studies and personal development that I had at Dallas while I was at Graterford. I was resolved not to let any incident cloud my route to parole, so I spelled out my plans in the "Book of Life." For the board to recognize, receiving my culinary arts program diploma would be a reliable mark on my resume.

You could find me labouring in the field, grinding on a tractor, or turning cow poop into compost when I wasn't in class or the library. Even though I would have never in a million years assumed that cow dung would bring me happiness, it was nice to be alone in the fresh air and enjoy the little things in life. It served as a gentle reminder that you can swiftly transform bullshit into something worthwhile if you possess the drive to do so.

CHAPTER 19
IMPLEMENTS OF ESCAPE

I asked a guard I got along with in SCI Graterford in 2010 if I could keep my cell a transit cell, meaning that only guys who were staying for a week or two before being sent to another prison would be housed in it. I asked for this because I knew that if any of the men stayed, it would make sure that I never grew too comfortable and that the movement would serve as a constant reminder that my time here was also temporary.

When you're incarcerated, you try your hardest to break out from the routine. There's a protracted denial phase during which you try to find ways to maintain what little agency you still have and dissociate yourself from the prison system because you can't believe this is your reality. You look for ways to normalise the experience as much as you can. Ironically, the moment you start to normalise the experience, you start to accept the pattern and eventually become at ease.

It would keep me from getting too comfortable to have different cellmates, but it would also give me some sidewalk therapy, stories from beyond the cell. Upon receiving a new cellie, my first thought would always be, "Damn, you cool man, do you need anything?" In the end, the guy told me stories about the free world that made me think about life outside since he was still digesting what had happened to him. Your cellie gets more at ease and starts to open up to you about their lives outside of prison. This gives you greater insight into what life is like outside the prison walls.

You become a person's therapist once you have assisted them through those initial days when they require assistance making phone calls, purchasing smokes, and applying makeup and they have seen that you are not trying to take advantage of them. They will begin to discuss their relationships with their side chicks in addition to their spouses. They would tell me stories about their travels to Miami and Los Angeles, including the types of automobiles they drove, the restaurants they frequented, the NBA games they attended, the clubs they frequented, the movies they saw, the colour of the interior of their car, and the menu items they ordered at eateries. And because I was so engrossed in these tales, I would become an interrogator, pressing the most precise inquiries in order to elicit the most thorough responses.

While strolling across the yard one day in 2011, I noticed this small neighbourhood youngster. I contacted his mother because I knew her and told her that I had seen her son and would be watching for him. Considering that he was about to enter prison, I made sure he had access to makeup, clean underwear, and other necessities. While we were creating together, engaging in my kind of sidewalk therapy, he introduced me to Google.

You have to remember that the internet wasn't what it is today and that everything in the outside world happened much faster quickly while I was incarcerated from 2002 to the present. He explained to me that Google is essentially a search engine that can look up anything. I thought he was full of baloney the entire time I was listening to him. In certain cases, the skill of distorting the truth transforms imprisoned niggas into adept yoga practitioners; in other cases, guys become creative due to their discontent with reality; and in still other cases, people are just talking nonstop. When he told me this, I assumed the young kid was acting in this manner.

"I can even investigate you."

This young guy thinks I'm slow because I've been in prison for so long.

"How the fuck can you look me up on some shit that I wasn't out in the free world for?" I ask the young bull.

This was prior to jails having access to the internet. We got all the information we needed from buying books, going to the library, or watching television, so I had to trust the young bull when he told me things I felt were fiction. It wasn't until maybe a few years later, in 2013, that my man Frank Nitty (RIP) showed up in my cell one day with an iPod Touch and a Clear wifi hotspot. My mind was blown since up until now, all I had ever seen of this garbage was on television.

"How in the hell are you going to use this?" Frank was the one I asked.

He's now telling me that he uses it to google crap, watch porn, and listen to music. I've been there for eleven years at this point, so looking at porn was the first thing that came to mind. However, I initially entered my name into Google to determine if the young bull was speaking the truth.

How the hell about it?

I let go of the iPod when I saw my name appear. I was so afraid that I assumed the federal government was watching me. I was afraid this Google garbage was going to give me more access than I wanted, but when I got over my first worry and spent that night in my cell, I started to consider what else I could use it for. I approached Frank about getting an iPod at that point.

I'll disclose how I acquired the iPod, but I won't reveal who outsider gave it to me in order to protect the innocent. I once instructed a guest to put their iPod Touch and wireless hotspot in the garbage bin at the foot of the hill. I was cleaning up outside at this time after all the other prisoners had gone inside. I instructed the user to dispose of the hot spot and iPod Touch like usual trash by placing them in a McDonald's bag. After picking up the trash for the compound down there, I went upstairs and got connected.

I had no idea that using the iPod and wireless hotspot would become a means of escape when I first bought them. An act of escape in prison is a crime that accuses you of possessing items that could let you physically break out of prison on some kind of life-or Shawshank Redemption-style scheme. However, I was utilising it as a mental diversion. I used to spend a lot of time there researching, watching Les Brown, YouTube courses, and of course, porn. My friend Nitty gave me my golden ticket to freedom in the most improbable of places—the trenches of a maximum-security jail. Life has a funny way of tossing you curveballs. I don't know if Nitty knew that he had unexpectedly saved my life, but I will always be appreciative of the instrument he gave me that would make a huge difference in my life.

"You're a real jerk, Steve Jobs. I clutched the tiny computer in the palm of my hand and murmured, "Thank you, sir. I was taken months at a time to a place far beyond the barbed wire barriers that limited our understanding of the outside world. This little device, which patrol might have used to find me and ruin my life, provided me with countless games and intelligence that allowed me to interact with my future self in ways I never could have imagined. In addition to learning a ton of stuff via YouTube, one of the benefits of the internet was that it allowed me to talk to anyone, anywhere, at any time.

Conversely, my passion for the advantages of having technology at my fingertips led me to pursue a career in telecoms. That is referred to as "hustling cell phones" in the workplace. I called around Philadelphia using a third-party software to find a plug that would bring up iPhones and iPods for me to sell, even if it was dangerous. I felt like I could do anything when that started.

I would blow up Cousin Gillie's phone whenever I had the chance, brainstorming ideas for stuff we could put together as soon as I set foot on solid land. Every call served as a template for our plans and aspirations. These weren't your normal calls either; we weren't interested in discussing what was happening on the streets or within the beast's gut. From filming advertisements to designing garments, we drew out big plays. Everything from the thread count we would employ to every other detail was discussed. Not only was the iPhone a piece of technology, but it served as our main office.

Every night, hiding cell phones was a high-stakes game. It was not always easy to pass off contraband to other cellmates, but when the benefits outweighed the potential risks, it was a decision that was easy to make. It seemed like I was sleeping close to ticking time bombs the nights I had the stockpile. It was a risky dance, balancing on the edge of nervousness and excitement, to see who texted or contacted you late at night when you couldn't answer the phone.

On September 14, 2013, I discovered that I had twenty-two missed calls when I woke up. As I stealthily glanced at the broken, pixelated screen of an iPhone 4, I couldn't help but think that something had to be wrong. One thing I know for sure is that nothing positive ever happens or comes of good news after a certain hour on the clock. As I gazed at the missed call log, my thoughts immediately turned to my grandma. My biggest worry was that my nanny wouldn't survive to see me leave. I ignored the disturbing thought, shaking my head in denial. I had not spent much time in the dayroom, so I felt as though my body was floating as I moved there.

The TV screen displayed Channel 6 news, with the noise down to a near silence. I could only make out the awning covering a doorway on a block that bore a striking resemblance to Nanny's. I pleaded, "Turn it up, turn it up," to get the volume upped. The speaker's words, "At one forty AM, a thirty-nine-year-old Black man was the fatal victim of gunshot wounds, one in his stomach, the other in his head," still echo in my mind as if they were spoken yesterday.

My ears suddenly felt as though they were full of water, and I heard a scream unlike anything I had ever heard come out of my soul. I knew without hearing anything else that my brother Steven had died.

My godsister was the first person I called to confirm the information. I wanted to be sure that this was real before telling Nanny or my mom about it, so I refrained from calling them right away. I didn't want to inflict any more heartbreak because Stevie and I had already caused enough. I realised this was real when my godsister instructed me to phone home.

When I eventually reached Nanny, she informed me that she heard gunfire after Steve had gone to the gas station around the block to grab a candy bar. When she got to the door, she saw Steve dash across the street and then pass out inside the house. He fell into her arms as soon as he entered. What happened? Nanny told me she asked him. Who fired at you? He raised his head to face her, and just as he appeared to be about to speak, his eyes rolled to the back of his head. In Nanny's arms, Stevie passed away. The way he died broke my heart. Not only was my brother abused, but my grandmother also needed to witness it.

I called my mom after I hung up with Nanny, and all I could remember was her saying, "They took my baby!" and these visceral cries. And I'm thinking, Superman was killed by these niggas. People assumed that because I was wilder, I would pass away before him, but here I was, outliving my superman.

CHAPTER 20
ONCE AGAIN IT'S ON

I had been a free man for 4,215 days, and I had 1,143 days still to go until I was free once more. It was during my six months of solitary confinement that I came to this realisation.

State troopers broke into our cells without warning, searching for illegal stuff. I was later accused of having firearms or other escape devices and contraband. Put another way, the three cell phones, five chargers, five headsets, iPod, and wireless hotspot I had hidden were all found by the troopers. I must have been the target of a snitch. It sent me down to the hole.

Strangely enough, the result of being in isolation ended up being exactly what I really needed. That brief period of confinement was strangely transforming for me. Unaware of it, my refusal to accept my brother's death had caused me to regress in several areas and go back into old habits. I lost touch with my feelings and became cold toward both people and myself. Confronting the grief that had been plaguing me since September 14, 2013, the day my hero received his wings, was unattainable for me due to denial.

Being trapped in that frigid box for so long pushed me to confess my sins, extend forgiveness, grieve, and let go of the anguish I had been carrying around for so long was a strange but fortunate experience. I was able to confront the pain I could not let go of during those alone hours since the system had robbed me of the opportunity to say goodbye to my Steven and send him on his way. I was able to properly grieve for my elder brother's passing in the depths of loneliness, finally make sense of the confusing web that had persisted since my father vanished, and finally feel at peace.

Another wake-up call came to me in the quiet of that storm, when an inner voice pushed me to consider the pain all of this had caused my mother—pain that I myself had caused, my selfishness making me resent her for the weight of my father's absence and the unrealistic expectations I had of her to ease the suffering I was holding inside. I released her from the unjustified weights I had put on her. I shed tears as a revelation came to me just when I needed it. I released myself psychologically by whispering, "I love you, Mom," through tears. I cherish you!

Appearing before the parole board was like entering a combat zone. You can never be sure which strategy the other board members will employ to weaken and attack you and your persona, no matter how well-prepared and armoured you are. No amount of planning will protect you from their scrutiny, but I felt strong and ready to confront them with my raw truth and take any conclusions they would draw. I felt content with who I was and the path I'd taken to become the finest version of myself.

The board members had gloomy expressions on their faces, and nothing I said appeared to change that. When I brought up my progress, they were dismissive, gruff, and occasionally frigid.

"Well, sir, I've attended twelve-step programs, earned a culinary certification, finished my GED, but more than that, I've led study groups and workshops that have helped a number of men better understand life's realities, like—" But before I could say anything further, I was interrupted by another sharp query.

Parole Commissioner: Umm, it says here that you were found guilty of possession of contraband and weapons or implements of escape and were sentenced to disciplinary transfer and solitary confinement. What have you to say to that?

Inmate Peeples: I'd say I was guilty of possessing cell phones and their accessories, but they were not used negatively or for any thought of escape.

Parole Commissioner: What exactly were they used for then, Mr. Peeples?

Inmate Peeples: Well, Commissioner, my mission today was to be fully transparent and accountable, so if I am being sincere, I did a lot of research through YouTube on different businesses I could start if you offered me parole; I created a social media page @Wallo267 where I post positive messages about staying out of prison. You can look it up yourself and see. Oh, and porn. I did watch a good amount of porn, Commissioner.

A MOMENT OF SILENCE DEscended upon the chamber, and the members of the board began to stand differently. I felt light as a feather and prepared to confront whatever route their verdict took me, even though I wasn't sure whether I had gone too far and revealed too much unvarnished truth.

My closing remarks felt the same as the conversations I had with myself in the pit. The man I previously was had no applause to show for the long list of community service I planned to perform or the admission of regret I'd come to know. All you could hear was the tick-tock of the wall-mounted clock, and you could almost hear a pin drop.

The guard pushed me up against the wall and frisked me for weapons—as if he hadn't already done so multiple times—before signalling for the automatic door to open and escorting me back inside the hearing room after a brief break. Really, what was I supposed to do, dig up a hidden cell phone hoard and throw it at someone? For once, all I wanted was to be respected for the man I'd grown into, not taken advantage of at every turn as I begged to be free.

The atmosphere in the room remained as strained as it had been at the beginning of the hearing. I almost regretted being so transparent and keeping my word to never filter anything. I wondered if I could have played checkers instead of chess with them. To tell the truth, though, I wasn't even playing a game. I realised that in order to honour the journey I had been on, I had to be true to who I was when I arrived.

Parole Commissioner: We've reconvened for the hearing of the panel's decision in the matter of Mr. Wallace Peeples. He is serving a 13.5 to 27-year sentence for armed robbery in the first degree. For the record, Mr. Peeples, this decision has not been easy for us. We were torn between the habitual past behaviours and the evidenced behavioural rehabilitation noted throughout your records. This decision was difficult with respect to the crimes committed and the lack of regard for human dignity. Although you may have absolved some issues personal to yourself during your sentence, it does not diminish the viciousness of the crimes you've committed against your community. With that said, the crucial question our panel must answer is whether you are still a potential threat to public safety. We have found the sufficient recording of reformative conduct and complete acceptance of your responsibility for your crimes to deem you suitable for parole.

Tears suddenly flooded my face. The commissioner went on with her closing remarks, but in my mind, I had already broken free from my chains and exited the room.

The commissioner yelled, "Mr. Peeples."

"Yes, sir," I replied as I turned back to look at the panel.

"Off the record, you balanced an otherwise impassed choice with your candour, sincerity, and willingness to become creative in serving the people. You have limitless potential, so please take use of the board's grace.

I committed myself to teaching everyone who would listen over the course of the next ninety days about what needed to be done in order to be fit for release. I turned it up to the point where, everytime I walked into the room, I could hear some of the guys laughingly saying, "Aw shit, here comes Pastor Peeples." That didn't matter, though. I cracked the code. I lifted the curse. Making amends for my transgressions was crucial to my release and continued sobriety.

Unexpectedly, getting busted with cell phones, which had appeared to be my biggest mistake, ended up being a godsend. The unanticipated transfer caused my sentence to be recalculated, which resulted in the removal of a whole year. Praise be to God for the internet! It was the impetus for my salvation as well as the path that took me to the depths of my extreme metamorphosis!

I entered the land of the free on Saturday, February 18, 2017, after passing through the hell's chained gates.

My lungs felt the coolness of the fresh air differently. That was an illusion of separation, I thought, even though we were in the open yard, and the air between us was still heavy with the heartbreaking tales of thirty-five hundred men behind bars. I thought to myself as I peered out the transport bus's foggy window, "Today is the day my life will begin!"

CHAPTER 21
ARMED WITH GOOD INTENTIONS

I got to work as soon as the excitement of my welcome-home parties subsided. When I first started using social media, I shared a video of $1,000 strewn on a bed in the middle room at Nanny's house. I unfolded the pages of the "Book of Life" and positioned it such that my iPhone's lens could see it. I said, "Peep game, this is one thousand in cash," as I hit the record button and faced the camera. I just left the prison on Saturday morning, as you can see. With the help of this legitimate game in this book and the thousand that you are currently viewing, I plan to transform this thousand into a hundred grand. That hundred will become a million, and that million will become a hundred million thanks to my actions. What am I going to do, you know? In addition to providing for my family, I intend to create riches that will last generations. You can accomplish it if I can. It's only been a few days since I returned home, but I'm going to show up. You can do anything if you can see it, so never let someone tell you that you can't.

I was released from prison seven days later on February 24.

While many were just interested in witnessing the spectacle, some believed that I had gone insane. Before I even had faith in myself, Cousin Gillie had to put a stop on me and set me straight on one issue before our mission began.

Bruce Springsteen's "Streets of Philadelphia" was one of the tunes I listened to repeatedly on my headphones. I was running the streets when this song first came out, and even then, I remember how well it encapsulated what it was like to live in Philadelphia. I was about fourteen at the time.

Bruce sings in the jawn about feeling defeated, not being able to identify his own face in the mirror, and walks till he loses feeling in his legs. Upon returning home, I was essentially by myself. I would be exploring the city on my own, strolling up and down Broad Street in the downtown area. All I had with me was my book bag, my headphones, and a few bucks in my pocket to cover the cost of the bus ride.

I became aware that I was having trouble with the material on other people's timelines when I started making my inspirational films in and around Philadelphia and sharing them on Instagram after I moved out. One thing about grabbing people's attention that I did understand was that you have to make them laugh in order to get them to listen. Social media is a game of attention. I had to be able to make them forget about their thumbs since their attention span is only about eight seconds, and once they remembered, they started scrolling again.

Real Street Talk was a program that I participated in when I was incarcerated. The idea behind the program was to allow those of us who were already serving time to offer some games to the incoming inmates in the hopes that some of them would view this as a chance to turn their lives around. I used to speak in front of groups of one or two hundred men as one of the speakers for Real Street Talk. With their fervour, intensity, and distinct perspective, so many of my widely shared Instagram videos have their roots in Real Street Talk.

I don't really recall what I said, but I do recall that Brother Ali, one of the originals, was there. Brother Ali was always courteous and kept his distance. He was an elderly prisoner who had spent nearly forty years behind bars. Everyone in the prison had respect for him. However, he didn't actually talk to many people.

The cell adjacent to mine was occupied by Brother Ali. Ali phoned me into his cell following one of my conversations.

"What's going on?" As I stood at the doorway, I questioned him.

"Man, I got chills hearing you talk. brings up memories of Brother Malcolm's life. Since I'm an older brother, I can relate. However, the young males also get it. You have a humorous and wise voice. You speak so quickly and smoothly. You had better use that gift when you get home.

The Malcolm X connection may make some people roll their eyes, but seeing someone who was close to Malcolm and had seen him speak compared me to him gave me a boost. That's where the inspiration for those videos came from—the ones where I was seen laying on the ground with ketchup on my forehead, racing around in the rain while wearing socks, and advising people, "Don't wait until it's too late." I was a guy possessed, and some people thought differently.

While I'm visiting my cousin Gillie one day, he receives a call from someone we both know lives in the same neighbourhood. He doesn't know I'm there when he phones Gillie, so he starts babbling about my vids.

Hey, dude, what's wrong with your cousin? Is he doing okay? That guy is insane, man.

The fact that I could tell he didn't get the message by the way he was laughing troubled me more than his laughter itself. He didn't appear to care who I was talking to or why I was saying things; he just seemed to react to the way I was saying them.

"Nope, because ain't crazy," Gillie answered. "Just going about his business." He is taking care of him.

Gil turned to face me after hanging up. "I'm not going to lie, because. I don't know what you were doing, but I knew you weren't playing around in the streets with no sense. You didn't come home upset, you didn't come on furious, or anything like that. I had to help you, then. Continue doing what you're doing," he added.

Guys who have served time in prison often have low energy levels when they return home. After a bid, they come home feeling as though they've won a PhD from college. They anticipate being commended for returning home, and they frequently become bitter when those same individuals who may have formerly complimented them go on in life.

Being entitled was the last thing I was going to allow myself to feel after witnessing how easily well-meaning intentions might send me back to a cage. I reflected on how my frustration after losing that dice game in 2002 caused me to serve fifteen years in prison. I was eager to accomplish anything simple. My thoughts were brief. I would have saved my penny and bought some penny candy if you had told me to risk a penny to win a million dollars and that I would be selling T-shirts for $20 or $25.

Gillie was accurate. I hadn't given it that much thought. I thought I needed to become a wordsmith in order to convey my new message of transformation and positivism because I had fought so hard to change the image I once had. However, "Fuck that!" From the bottom up, the streets that formerly witnessed my suffering will now see unadulterated will and fortitude.

I didn't start out with the intention of making money. I used every dollar I made to further the objective, even though I needed money to survive first and to market and promote myself second. I started selling T-shirts and merchandise out of the trunk on the street after purchasing an outdated, beat-up minivan as a means of transportation. I acquired a website domain, formed an LLC, and registered my name Wallo267 as a trademark with the money I made. The number "267" is derived from my jail ID. Being institutionalised has caused me to identify my identity with the terms used to refer to me. My name stuck after I heard the numerals followed by my name for years.

My mother and I had a bond that grew stronger during my new adventure, serving as a pillar of support and stability for me when I reached unimaginably high points in my development. Whenever she would bring Steven's daughter and son, my niece Princess MayMay and my nephew Mukson, to visit me in prison, we would often think back on the conversations we had during those trips. They all contributed significantly to my ability to stay committed to my objectives. However, Princess MayMay, my infant daughter, made the deal.

She had once told him, "Uncle, you have to be good when you get out of here, so you never come back and leave me." The loving factors that strengthened me to spread that love to the four corners of every neighbourhood were those seeds they planted and watered.

It was only twenty months after returning home that I received an invitation to give a speech on the widely popular TED Talks program. Real estate investor Nicole Purvy had a sister who worked with children out of her place in North Philadelphia, which was close to all the drug addiction and other activities going on, especially down in the Badlands. Nicole was among those who not only observed what I was doing, but also showed admiration for the strategy I employed to try to reach the most vulnerable members of society. When I went to visit her one day, she told me about her brother Jabari from Atlanta who was organising TEDx lectures. He found out about my page from Nicole, and he thought my offerings were special for their platform.

A nonprofit organisation called TED invites some of the most creative and powerful minds to spread their expertise to a wider audience. Although the movies are typically around twenty minutes long, they cover a wide range of subjects and have a worldwide audience. Although the TEDx speeches took place in a more regional setting, the official affiliation indicated that my Instagram strategy was effective. I was doing speeches at this time for honoraria, like

$600 here, $1,000 there. When they ask, I will go. I realised that this possibility went beyond financial gain when Nicole described it to me because it offered me the potential to reach a wider audience on a platform that isn't usually used by individuals from my hometown. I was both nervous and excited about the possibility since I could see that my demographic reach was growing rapidly. The main topics the event planner recommended were a discussion about life in jail and beyond, but my heart had other ideas. It would take guts to speak to a larger audience in order to remove the curtain and shed light on a generally gloomy environment when seeking retribution is accepted as the only viable course of action.

Jabari set for a flight for me to travel to Buckhead, Atlanta, where the event was being held, after I told him I was down. I watched a ton of various films before to get a sense of the format and see what unique perspective or ideas I might provide. I treated this as a rap fight, pretty much. friendly rivalry. I wanted to make sure that I chose a topic that people would not just listen to, but also feel, because I knew that no one would be as passionate and energetic as myself.

That night, I had seven minutes to make an impression on a group of people who might not have realised the differences that come with being a resident of an underprivileged area. With more than 31.9 million TED Talks viewers on YouTube, I felt I only had one chance to share the most important testimony of my life. I inhaled deeply and then released my chest to say, "I forgive my brother's killer."

I felt betrayed, scared, and abused when I learned that Steven had died in September of 2013. I'm still not sure who killed my brother or why, to this day. I discovered that in circumstances such as those, you never receive the whole story.

I felt exposed at the moment as well because it seemed like everyone was staring at me. Because of the street mindset I was raised in and the fact that others in my neighbourhood knew my brother, there was an implicit expectation that I ought to take action.

Retaliation and revenge are powerful drivers of the cycle of crime, demise, and jail in inner cities across America. The only thing that makes sense when someone takes away one of your loved ones is to have them experience the same level of grief as you. I also realised that the message of forgiving someone's killer would only be effective because it came from me, who was living what I preached, and that those who refrain from taking revenge are frequently viewed as weak. Advice on surviving the ghetto is frequently given by those who aren't going through the same things, so hearing it from someone who hasn't been there is like hearing someone who only played junior varsity basketball try to tell you how to get into the NBA.

I had to extend forgiveness to someone who had stolen my brother, my niece's and nephew's father, and my mother's son. I was motivated to take action because I was aware of the large number of people abusing the powerful narcotics of hatred and retribution in order to numb the painful reality of bereavement. I vowed to myself not to get even with the man who kidnapped my brother. I believe that the fact that I would never know who it was was really beneficial since it made me face my pain's vulnerability head-on without any outside distractions.

Before I was able to forgive my brother's killer, I shared the belief held by many that showing forgiveness meant that I was letting someone off the hook or that I was allowing them to get away with anything. Had I not shown forgiveness to the man who killed my brother, I most likely would have been hunting him down, attempted his murder, and ended myself dead or incarcerated. I was reminded of this entire process when I heard Jay-Z discuss how his father abandoned the family in order to find the person who killed his brother, Jay-Z's uncle. According to Jay, his father develops a heroin addiction while on the warpath, and they don't get back together for decades. I asked myself if I wanted to take away from the people I cared about even more than they had already lost while I was incarcerated. After I did, I understood that forgiving myself was a gift I was giving to myself since it allowed me to move on with my life. I allowed myself to be alive.

Early in the morning of February 2019, I saw this Variety article headlined "Spotify Buys Podcast Startups Gimlet Media and Anchor, Plans Up to $500M in Acquisitions in 2019". The report states that Spotify intended to invest between $400 million and $500 million in podcasts in that specific year. I'm going to call Gil now that I'm awake.

I told him, "Yo nigga, read this article," as his voicemail sounded.

He didn't answer at first since he was sleepy. After I've made around ten calls, he tells me he will read it when he wakes up. Then he called me back.

Hey, this must be completed. Let's finish this up.

We handled intellectual property, trademark counsel, and other legal matters by April, at which point we launched the first episode of Million Dollaz Worth of Game. In the first seven hours, we shot up to number two in comedy and number four overall in the podcast charts. Naturally, these people inspired me to keep going, but I was surprised. Until then, I had never seen the consequences of what I had done materialise so rapidly. When you release something new, you can never be sure how people will respond. I also made myself stop believing that things would be easy so that I wouldn't walk through locked doors. Even though those numbers were announced seven hours after Gil and I published our first episode, it took me thirty-nine years to grasp the kind of influence I might have. However, what began as an enjoyable means of interacting with others worldwide and engaging in humorous discussions on frequently difficult topics and transformative circumstances via our podcast evolved into a breakthrough success in a market that was overloaded with millions of episodes.

The success of our show opened doors we never would have imagined. Our energy and dynamic as loyal brothers, cousins, and friends changed the traditional tough-guy atmosphere in hip-hop and cities all over the world. True love, affection, and the ability to trash talk each other without ever feeling like there is a trace of contempt shown are almost unheard of—unless it's in a funny way. Together, we broke that mould, ending another generational curse.

Our childhood dreams of becoming a hip-hop group that toured the world evolved with the times. They brought us into a platform that allowed us to advocate for underrepresented groups in Philadelphia, Los Angeles, and the United Kingdom. We've become a globally recognized brand because of our volunteer work and charity undertakings. I hate to boast, but the podcast deal we worked out with Barstool Sports was one of the biggest of its sort. We came together out of goodwill and good intentions, and we not only established creative control over a really unlikely group (they are very White, and we are quite Black). In addition, after the epidemic, we combined our resources and invested $4.5 million to help affected small companies.

I now frequently use the phrase "armed with good intentions" in my speech. Learning to be resourceful and build stronger relationships with people were two things I did after realising I was more capable than I had thought. Reflection helped me realise that I can succeed in anything I set my mind to. And that insight allowed me to make the most of my good intentions, which have always been my greatest strength. I've learned that if you truly want to be totally changed, you have to be incredibly intentional!

The most of my crazy past actions, the crimes that have kept me imprisoned in perilous situations for the most of my life, were, in one way or another, driven by good intentions. Yes, I wanted to be the head of my household and provide for my family and others, but I also wanted the flashy things that made people smile, especially the great people in Philadelphia. My only motivation for partaking in foolish actions and trying to live a life that was out of character was the desire to be a part of something greater and better than what I experienced on the seedy streets of Philadelphia.

There were days when I wanted to forget about it, give up, or worse. I missed the days when I could just curl up in my bunk and take those naps that never seemed to end. You know, the ones from which one can never truly escape. But the thoughts never lasted more than a minute or so because there was always a voice, maybe God's voice, or whatever it was, telling me to never give up.

I used to cry silently to myself every day, "No one will save you." This statement acted as a constant reminder that my objective encompassed love for everyone, wherever on the earth, in addition to my family and myself. And I needed to get better for those people.

I have changed as a man; I have a new perspective and an unquenchable drive to continue developing so that I can conquer my circumstances and the conditions of others. I've proven my resilience by being put to the test! I have no mercy when it comes to accomplishing my objective. My whole life has been committed to using my experiences to inspire others to press on, no matter how challenging or hopeless things may seem along the path. Over the years, I've witnessed more folks who are regrettably paralyzed by fear of their past. I'm guessing that their negative mindset hindered them more than being incarcerated. But the themes of this book are persistence and the resolve to face the days ahead while staying completely true to who you are.

I want you to know that no matter what—whether you're feeling stuck or facing insurmountable challenges—you can conquer anything, just like I did. You just need to never give up on yourself.

The story in this book is of how I went from being a scared, disturbed, and seemingly lost young man to a man of integrity and hope, from terrorising the streets of Philadelphia to being acknowledged by the mayor as a change agent and valuable member of the community that raised me. This has not at all been easy or appealing. Still, it was real and vulnerable.

CHAPTER 22
REFORMED

PRESS RELEASE: February 13, 2024
REFORM Alliance Appoints Wallace "Wallo267" Peeples to Serve as Organization's New
Chief Marketing Officer
NEW YORK, FEB. 13, 2024 /PRNEWSWIRE/ – Today, REFORM Alliance formally
announces the appointment of Wallace "Wallo267" Peeples to lead the organisation's
marketing department as Chief Marketing Officer. Peeples will be responsible for the
development of REFORM's long-term marketing strategy, activations, and brand
innovation. Peeples will play a critical role as the organisation continues to further its
commitment to transform supervision by changing laws, systems, and culture to create real
pathways to work and well-being.

MEEK MILL IN LATE 2023 Give me a FaceTime.

Hey, what's going on? Mike Rubin gave me a call and informed me that they may include you in REFORM's marketing efforts.

The nonprofit organisation known as REFORM Alliance was established by Meek Mill, Jay-Z, American investor Michael Novogratz, social justice activist Clara Wu Tsai, hedge fund manager Daniel S. Loeb, and Michael Rubin, the CEO and founder of Fanatics, a global digital sports platform. The laws pertaining to probation, parole, and sentencing—all of which I have personally experienced—are the main emphasis of REFORM. I didn't think twice when Meek informed me that I would be managing the marketing for a company that put in a lot of overtime for folks just like me.

Mike Rubin told Meek he thought of me as a one-man advertising campaign. He approved of the way I conveyed my message and marketed my businesses. I log on and take care of it on my own.

When Mike approached Jay-Z and Meek about offering me the job, they both thought it would be a fantastic idea.

It was encouraging to hear how much faith everyone had in me. I told Meek, "Hell yeah," and Mike reached out to me personally two days after. He texted his executive assistant and me. I then met with Des, my business manager. They treated her with respect, which I found admirable and moved by. As I've advanced in my career, I've witnessed the subtly negative ways in which individuals disparage those of us who they perceive to be less successful than themselves. They make tiny mistakes like sending me messages after I've told them to contact Des or forgetting to include others in emails. It was, therefore, crucial to me that they gave Des what I believed she was due.

We first met at Fanatics to discuss what it would be like to join REFORM.

Wallo, listen up," Mike said to me. "You are an excellent marketer. You establish a connection, a connection with those we wish to reach. It's real, you're organic, and you are raw. It's not compulsory. At REFORM, we require you to serve as our chief marketing officer. How does that appear to you?

I didn't expect to run the entire division; all I thought I was going to do was go there and campaign. However, I studied this while incarcerated. The fact that I am qualified under this title alone serves as my testament to my expertise. I went from wearing ketchup on my head and warning people, "Don't wait until it's too late," as a viral stunt to receiving an offer for a corporate position, so that meeting was quite emotional for me. Despite not having an MBA or a college degree, here I am.

This meeting gave the folks the world has forgotten about—as well as myself—validation. I always feel like I speak for them—the folks who might be homeless or live in run-down neighbourhoods, the individuals who have served time in prison, the people who have failed in life, and the ones who are struggling with drug addiction. I felt incredibly strong, as if I was showcasing our accomplishments to them. The options following incarceration are the options following failure. It's the opportunity to triumph following a setback.

Mike went on, "I don't want all of your time because I know you got a lot going on." After a few months, Des and I visited Mike's crib outside of Philadelphia on a Saturday morning. The house was incredible, and I only needed half of your time to be able to stay on top of things and truly bring this to reality. Within the gate were a lake, a bridge, a tennis court next to a basketball court, and a swimming pool. On the first day of February, I started working as the CEO after we met with Robert Rooks, who is one of my favourite guys—honest, sincere, and genuinely cared about the individuals that the world forgot about. Robert broke down everything.

I know anything is possible when I consider that I was assigned to REFORM only a few weeks before my release's seventh anniversary. Even though I have twenty-four years before I'm released from parole at the age of forty-five, I am thankful that I have already overcome so many obstacles. And each year goes by faster than the last. Every year brings me one step closer to regaining my freedom.

Observe me. additionally YouTube's cultural advisor. I am grateful that Lyor Cohen and Tuma Basa saw potential in me. After terrorising the area, I took one of the largest platforms in the world and set up shop in other communities throughout the nation, teaching people how to launch their own YouTube channels, grow their followings, and make money from their channel. All from YouTube Avenues, a show I co-created with my team and which has already travelled to several cities, including Philadelphia, Atlanta, Houston, Oakland, Washington, D.C., Baltimore, and New Orleans. All stemming from an idea I had to develop a program to teach our folks how to win on YouTube and how YouTube functions. Take a look at me!

The contents of this book may not be copied, reproduced or transmitted without the express written permission of the author or publisher. Under no circumstances will the publisher or author be responsible or liable for any damages, compensation or monetary loss arising from the information contained in this book, whether directly or indirectly.

Disclaimer Notice:

Although the author and publisher have made every effort to ensure the accuracy and completeness of the content, they do not, however, make any representations or warranties as to the accuracy, completeness, or reliability of the content. , suitability or availability of the information, products, services or related graphics contained in the book for any purpose. Readers are solely responsible for their use of the information contained in this book

Every effort has been made to make this book possible. If any omission or error has occurred unintentionally, the author and publisher will be happy to acknowledge it in upcoming versions.

Made in United States
Orlando, FL
15 October 2024

52712597R00070